Measuring the Digital World

Using Digital Analytics to Drive Better Digital Experiences

Gary Angel

Publisher: Paul Boger
Editor-in-Chief: Amy Neidlinger
Executive Editor: Jeanne Glasser
Development Editor: Natasha Wolmers
Cover Designer: Alan Clements
Managing Editor: Kristy Hart
Senior Project Editor: Lori Lyons
Copy Editor: Hansing Editorial
Proofreader: Debbie Williams
Senior Indexer: Cheryl Lenser
Senior Compositor: Gloria Schurick
Manufacturing Buyer: Dan Uhrig

© 2016 by Pearson Education, Inc.
Publishing as FT Press
Upper Saddle River, New Jersey 07458

For information about buying this title in bulk quantities, or for special sales opportunities (which may include electronic versions; custom cover designs; and content particular to your business, training goals, marketing focus, or branding interests), please contact our corporate sales department at corpsales@pearsoned.com or (800) 382-3419.

For government sales inquiries, please contact governmentsales@pearsoned.com.

For questions about sales outside the U.S., please contact international@pearsoned.com.

Company and product names mentioned herein are the trademarks or registered trademarks of their respective owners.

Printed in the United States of America

First Printing December 2015

ISBN-10: 0-13-419508-6
ISBN-13: 978-0-13-419508-7

Pearson Education LTD.
Pearson Education Australia PTY, Limited.
Pearson Education Singapore, Pte. Ltd.
Pearson Education Asia, Ltd.
Pearson Education Canada, Ltd.
Pearson Educación de Mexico, S.A. de C.V.
Pearson Education—Japan
Pearson Education Malaysia, Pte. Ltd.

Library of Congress Control Number: 2015951825

We all need a little pushing sometimes.
This book is dedicated to Grace, Isabella, and Ilise
(my wife and daughters) who, knowing I wanted to,
bugged me until I agreed to write a book.
They will probably make fun of my picture on the book jacket,
but given that it is about digital analytics,
none of them will likely ever read it.
Yet without them, it would never have been written.

Contents

Acknowledgments

There are countless people who have contributed to and helped shape my understanding of digital measurement over the course of almost two decades. There are too many to count and probably too many to remember. I can't not mention the small group of people who helped me build Semphonic, the digital analytics practice where nearly all of this thinking grew up and matured. Every person on that team is special to me. They helped build a company and practice that proved to be the central endeavor of my adult life, and almost without exception they have been good friends as well.

Outstanding among that truly wonderful group is, of course, my original partner and co-founder in that endeavor, Joel Hadary. No matter the intellectual interest of a journey, it's the people you travel it with that make it enjoyable. It's hard for me to imagine a better partner for building a company and creating a discipline.

Three early employees who have been with me now on this journey for more than a decade must also be mentioned. Paul Legutko, Phil Kemelor, and Jesse Gross have all contributed mightily not just to the practice we built, but also to the thinking and approaches laid out here. Paul has shaped so much of my thinking on analytics—particularly the problems of segmentation, selection, and bias—that's it hard for me to know where my thinking starts and his ends. To Phil I owe much of the broader picture that makes analytics more than number crunching and focuses it on people and problems and how to solve them. Jesse—who began with us right out of college knowing no more of digital analytics than I know of Sanskrit—has been at least a full partner in the exploration of voice of customer and its role in digital measurement.

The voice may be mine, but the ideas are, as often as not, theirs.

When I started in digital analytics, it was a tiny community. Like most tiny communities, its members were oddballs. The best kind of eccentrics. Lacking credentials and degrees, digital analytics was peopled by those willing to explore a discipline that offered neither safe position nor any clear path to success. That's often the best kind of people. It has been both a pleasure and privilege to grow up in that community. To argue, to fight, to learn, and to share with a group of people who actually love what they do and strive to do it better.

Thank you all.

About the Author

Gary Angel currently leads Ernest & Young's (EY) Digital Analytics Practice. EY acquired Gary's previous company, Semphonic, in 2013. As President and co-founder, Gary led Semphonic's growth from a two-person consultancy to one of the leading digital analytics practices in the Unites States. Voted the most Influential Industry Contributor by the Digital Analytics Association, Gary writes an influential blog (http://semphonic.blogs.com/semangel), has published numerous whitepapers on advanced digital analytics practice, and is a frequent speaker at industry events. Over the last two decades, he's helped create and advance the state-of-the-art in digital measurement.

Preface

Measuring the (Digital) World

How do we understand the world around us? It's not so obvious.

Our senses feed a never-ending stream of data into our brains. In its raw form, that data is incredibly complex. Shapes, surfaces, sizes, shades, motions, scents, textures—we absorb them all, seemingly without effort. Even the most powerful supercomputers yet developed cannot begin to compete in real time. But the plastic mind of human babies—with the help, no doubt, of some careful pre-wiring—can learn how to make sense of this data, parse it, and react swiftly and intelligently to this tidal surge of information.

For centuries, philosophers have understood that the very existence of a world outside ourselves is impossible to verify. We know the world only from the inside, from the endless, constant processing we call consciousness and the apparent flow of data that we believe is generated by our eyes, ears, nose, and fingers. That such a thing as the physical world exists is beyond our ability to seriously doubt. But we know it only by interpreting essentially abstract data.

We grasp the world by imposing patterns on it—foundational patterns that have been imprinted and wired deep into our minds in the endless laboratory of nature. Size, shape, color, and motion are just a few of the core building blocks of our human understanding of the physical world. As fast as sense data funnels into the brain, we are contextualizing it, categorizing it along key dimensions, and then measuring and comparing everything.

That's the physical world. Evolution ensures that we know how to understand it, even if we don't know how we know. But the physical world is no longer the place where we spend all our time. We also live in the digital world, a world with different rules, different types of data, different frames of reference, and different types of measurement.

For the last 17 years, my job has been to measure the digital world. To glean, from the vast streams of data it showers upon us, the fundamental categorizations that matter. To develop the framing devices, dimensions, and measurements that let us understand this digital world with the same ease and power with which we parse the physical world around us. It's important work because we can shape and improve that world only when we understand how it works—not how it works from a programming perspective (although I started out as a programmer), but how it works for people.

These days, we spend immense amounts of time, energy, and money trying to improve the digital world. How well we do that work can determine the success and direction of public policy (healthcare. gov), the health of our love life (eHarmony), and the state of our knowledge about the world (nytimes.com).

This work isn't easy, and it isn't finished. We are still like newborn babes learning to parse the data from our digital sensors.

The digital world is fascinating. And unlike in the physical world, we have no pre-wiring for measuring and understanding the digital realm. Without that huge prebuilt advantage, our interpretations are wrong much more often than they are right. But when we get them right, we at least know what we did.

The pages that follow show you what we've learned so far about how to measure and understand the digital world.

1

Digital Meaning

We have tools dedicated to measuring the digital world. So it's no surprise that we assume the measurements those tools give us are the right ones for the job. They aren't. The standard set of web metrics most digital analytics tools use were developed long before people had even a basic understanding of how to do digital measurement, and mostly before analytics tools that could do much with the data were in widespread use.

The Digital Challenge: Our Metrics and Our Measurement Lack Meaning

The most common digital metrics are almost useless. They measure the wrong things in the wrong ways. They fail, at the most basic level, to link what happens in the digital world to our understanding of people's behavior. In this chapter, you identify the basic challenge of digital measurement and analytics, and you see why common metrics and reports can't easily answer the fundamental questions you're likely to ask about the digital world.

The Grocery Store with Invisible Patrons

Imagine a fairly normal grocery store, well stocked with cereal, milk, beer and wine, eggs, ice cream, canned goods, vegetables, fruits, and, of course, the usual assortment of treats near the register. Now imagine that the patrons and their carts are invisible. You see the door swing open when they arrive. You hear the cash register ring when they depart. You know what they bought. But everything else remains hidden. It would be hard to know how well the store was working and what you could do to make it better. Is it missing items or brands shoppers want? Is the store laid out in a way that makes life easy on customers? Does it maximize their purchasing behavior? Have you allocated the right amount of shelf space to each type of item? What might you do to get an individual customer to spend more or be more loyal?

These are the types of questions that merchandising experts have studied, pondered, and worked on for many years—since well before the digital world ever existed. Interestingly, they found that they could answer some of these questions even when the customers were, for all practical purposes, invisible. Equally interesting, they found that some types of questions are much harder to answer when you don't know who your customers are and that, for many questions, the data might suggest possible answers but rarely provides definitive guidance.

Suppose, for example, that you found that the most purchased items in your store were milk, beer, eggs, and chips. You might be tempted to move all these items together in one place right at the front of the store. That should make it easy for customers to find what they need quickly and efficiently. Is that the way your supermarket is laid out, with the items you buy most right up front?

Chances are, it's almost exactly the opposite. That isn't because you're invisible! Supermarkets work differently for two reasons. We're all deeply cynical consumers, so you probably identified the first reason right away. Groceries aren't set up for your convenience. They often place the things people purchase most at the very back of the store and might even consciously try to locate them far apart. If you've never made an impulse buy at a grocery store, this might seem odd. But if, like me, you've wandered by the dairy aisle and added some ready-to-bake cookies, or you've thrown a bag of chips next to your beer, it's not too hard to see why this setup works. By trying out different store layouts and measuring how much people buy (their average cart), store designers can maximize total sales. Mind you, most grocery stores count on you to make your decision about where to shop based on other factors than how long it takes you to get your items. They know price, selection, and location are more important than convenience. If a new grocery store opened right next door and had the same selection and same prices, a store might well compete on the convenience of layout. But most stores see their layout as a chance to maximize their profits, not your time.

The second reason grocery stores aren't laid out for your convenience is more interesting and more important than good old profit maximizing. Grocery stores have more than one customer. Guess what? They're all different. When grocery merchandisers began to study what people bought (still without knowing who they were— only what was purchased on the same ticket), they found very distinct patterns. Beer and milk might be two of the most commonly purchased items in a grocery store, but they might not often be purchased together. Chips, on the other hand, go pretty well with that beer. And milk buyers are often looking to add cereal or eggs to their cart. So setting up a grocery with the most purchased items all clustered together might not work particularly well or be particularly convenient for anyone.

What's more, even if a particular setup worked well for you today, it might not tomorrow. When merchandisers could only look at the receipts from each shopper, they had no way to tell how much people's habits and shopping patterns varied. That's a huge hole in their understanding. To get around that, grocery stores created loyalty programs so that, in return for discounts, they could tell what you bought every trip. They found that most people don't shop the same way every time they visit the grocery store. Most of us have regular shopping expeditions when we buy everything we need and go up and down every aisle. Store layout might not be a big deal when we're traversing every inch of the store (or, in my case, traversing two or three times as I remember things). But we also have visits when we've just run out of beer or milk—or, heaven forbid, both. We might stop to pick up lunch or to shop for specific recipe ingredients (my flour, bag of chocolate chips, vanilla extract, and egg visits). These are very distinct types of visits, and it would be great if the grocery store could make each type of visit perfect (or perfect for the grocer). Stores would love to be able to do that. But it's hard to push those shelves around when you walk in the door.

Let's not forget those chocolate bars and women's magazines perched right at the register. Very few of us go to the grocery store with the express intent of buying a Snickers bar and a *Cosmo*, but many of us are tempted by one or the other. What spot in the grocery store do people *have* to linger at with nothing to do but be tempted? That's where the candy (eye and stomach) goes.

We can learn a lot from those grocery store merchandisers when we start to think about the digital world. The straightest path isn't always the best. The customer's goals and your goals aren't always identical. Not every product is the same, and some products are more position sensitive than others. A store doesn't have one ideal layout because it doesn't have one type of customer, and customers aren't always going to do the same thing anyway. Last, and most important, what people actually do tells us a great deal about who they are and why they are doing those behaviors.

Getting Digital

We are blind to the digital world. Unassisted, we have no way of knowing whether our website is thronged with visitors or as empty as a mall after closing time, whether our cash registers are overflowing or stubbornly silent, whether our customers are young or old, whether our content is read with rapt attention or is barely and desultorily skimmed. We need eyes and ears to help us see into the digital world. Certain tools have that very function—to track and make visible the otherwise unseen patterns of that world. These digital analytics tools are powerful and rich. They include hundreds or thousands of possible reports and options that seem to expose every aspect of digital behavior. It's all too easy to forget how dependent we are on the exact nature of those tools and to assume that what they show us and the way they show it to us is all there is.

Our natural senses in the physical world have evolved to give us many advantages. We have adopted a deep and abiding faith in what we *see*. Yet even with our physical senses, it's all too easy to forget that the window they provide into the world is a narrow one.

Remember the image of a dress that went viral in early spring 2015? Many people see the dress as black and blue. Others see it as white and gold. If you look long enough or over some period of time, you might see it each way. If you didn't hear about the dress and you can't believe that anyone could see it differently than whichever way happens to strike you, check it out online and show it around. You'll be surprised.

Optical illusions are just one aspect of how our eyes can mislead us. We see color (no matter how much we might disagree about it), but we don't see heat.

Why should we see heat?

Well, why shouldn't we?

Infrared cameras see heat. It's just another wavelength, and for many purposes, seeing heat is far more useful than seeing light (when hunting at night, for example). For that matter, what if we could see radio waves? Hearing and vision seem fundamentally different to us, but each is a set of waves that different tools inside our body use.

What would our radio-wave eyes make of a Madonna song? Probably not much.

The simple fact is this: Our reality is constrained by the tools we experience it with.

What does all this have to do with digital analytics? The digital analytics tools we have are our windows into the digital world. We see only what they can track or think is important. We see what page a user requested from a server, but we don't see how long that page took to load. We see what link a user clicked on, but we usually don't see what part of the page that user scrolled to. We (sometimes) see what website the user came from, but we don't (usually) see what website that user went to. These choices make a profound difference in how we think about the digital world and what we tend to value as important there.

What if our tools aren't very good? What if the events they choose to capture or the ways they choose to show them to us give us only a shadowy impression of the real digital world or what's important inside it?

I've been around since the very beginning of digital analytics. I witnessed firsthand and, in some small ways, even helped shape how those digital tools evolved. Having seen their history, I know that the decisions about what to track in the digital world and how to track it were often ad hoc and shallow.

The first digital analytics tools were built to read weblogs. These logs weren't built to understand and measure the digital world. They were built to create a record of what a web server was doing so that IT professionals might be able to track down operational problems (although they were hardly ever used for that, either). These logs recorded IT-focused information about which content file was requested, when exactly it was processed, what IP address requested it, how much content was sent, and whether the request was successful.

Because those were the fields in the logs, those were the fields we used when we first built digital analytics tools. And being clever folk, we interpolated a whole lot from this bare bones little set of fields. We figured out a way to group the records by the device requesting them (which we promptly anthropomorphized into a human *visitor*). By looking at the time between requests, we could group the requests into batches by creating an arbitrary time limit, and we labeled these batches of requests *visits*. Then we could look at what page a visitor looked at first in that batch and we called that an entry page. We could also look at what page was last in the batch and call that an exit page.

It's important to realize just how arbitrary these decisions were. When a visitor first arrives on a website, that website sometimes records which website the visitor came from—this is called the referring site. By saving the referring site for each batch of records (a visit), you can get a sense of which sites are generating traffic to your pages. But here's a peculiarity: By defining an arbitrary time limit of 30 minutes to group records, we created situations in which a visit sometimes had more than one referring site; in other situations, a visit had a referring site that was the last page the visitor viewed on the same website.

For example, imagine that a visitor searches on Google or Bing, finds your website, and views a page. Then that visitor returns to the search engine, does another search, goes to a different site, and links from there to you within 30 minutes of the first request. You'll have a single visit with two referring sites. This might sound far-fetched, but in certain permutations, it's not uncommon. Many sessions will have multiple visits to Google interspersed with views of your pages.

It's even more likely, especially in our tabbed browser world (which came after all these definitions were created—you remember browsers without tabs, right?), that a visitor will view a page or tab elsewhere, spend some time there, and then return to your website and view another page. Same session? According to our tools, if that happens 25 minutes apart, it is. But if it happens 31 minutes apart, it isn't. And if it does happen 31 minutes apart, you'll have a whole new visit with a referring site of your own website!

It would have been perfectly plausible (maybe much more plausible) to decide that a batch of records should be separated by a referring site other than your own domain, regardless of time. But that's not the way some early vendors did it, so the definition stuck and became an artifact of truth.

And if a visit is merely a rough-and-ready and poorly defined artifact, then so are the entry page (the first page in a visit), the exit page (the last page in a visit), the visit time (the time between the first and last requests that are part of a visit), and the referring site (the domain recorded in the first record of the visit as the referrer, the site from which the user came)—all based on the way we defined a visit.

As with the words we read on a page, the numbers we see in a tool tend to take on privileged status in our minds. But if the only problem with standard web metrics were a certain sloppiness of definition, our situation wouldn't be all that bad. How much difference can it make whether a visit is defined by 30 minutes of inactivity or a new referring domain? Hard to say.

By showing how arbitrary these standard metrics are in construction, I hope to lessen their privileged status and make it easier to convince you that, not only are they arbitrary, but they are largely misguided.

Web measurement began with weblogs, whose goal was to measure digital assets. This long-ago bias has persisted through every generation of digital analytics tool. The implicit goal of analytics tools is to measure the website or the app. That's missing, if not the whole point, a big part of it. In the digital world, our goal should be to understand our customers, not our digital assets.

Our tools have improved to do that—probably more than our practice has. Digital analytics tools now deliver significant and interesting segmentation capabilities that enable you to define and track cohorts, segment on fairly complex behaviors, and compare different types of users. They even provide limited capabilities for integrating nondigital data into their reporting.

This is all good, and the technology seems to improve continually. But although the capabilities of the tools have improved, the basic views they provide haven't changed much. How many reports in a digital analytics tool tell you anything about customers? For that matter, how many of the digital reports you distribute in your organization have anything to do with customers? And how much do they really help you understand the digital world?

Close your eyes and picture your website. Imagine people of all sorts moving through it. They stop here or there. They go down certain pathways and ignore others. They look at this or that. They make a purchase or head for the exit. Can you see it?

Now open your web analytics tool. Do the reports help you visualize that scene? Do they help you understand who your customers are (beer and chips, or milk and eggs)? Can you find the different types of visits (going down every aisle, or just ran out of something) and see which are most common? Do they help you picture which customers do which visits most often (beer and chips, just ran out, Friday night)? In other words, do they actually help you understand the digital world or do they just confront you with a wall of numbers that elude meaning, even while seeming entirely plausible?

I first started measuring the digital world back when websites were brand new and people still talked about the World Wide Web. I'd spent the previous few years working with a couple large credit card companies, analyzing the way people use their credit cards to create marketing programs (yeah, sorry about all that crappy mail). We used some pretty fancy analysis techniques to group people together, to understand how they used their credit cards and then to classify them. It was pretty easy and powerful. It didn't take analytic genius to know that the cardholder who routinely dropped four figures at

Neiman Marcus was a different beast from that two-digit shopper at the local Walmart.

When I first got my hands on web behavioral data, I ran the same kind of (neural net) analysis and proudly sold the results. But whereas my credit card segmentations had truly been interesting and useful, my digital segmentations looked like some inverted Egyptian monstrosity (see Figure 1.1).

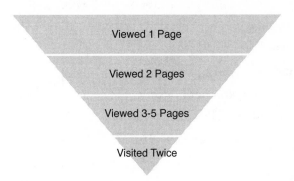

Figure 1.1 Inverted pyramid

Nobody ever got rich targeting "people who viewed 3–5 pages."

I spent years learning that the digital metrics tools provide aren't that interesting and that, no matter how powerful a tool I used to study digital behavior, I wouldn't get interesting results if I picked the wrong type of variables.

So put away your digital analytics tools for a minute. Forget all about page reports, referring sites, average page times, top exit pages, number of visits, average conversion rates, and the whole flavorless cornucopia of web metrics and reports that those tools spit out by default. It's all garbage in the most literal sense—it takes up mental space and it smells bad.

You're about to find a better way to understand the digital world.

2

Two-Tiered Segmentation

If all those traditional web metrics—such as page views, visits, and time onsite—aren't that useful, what is? This chapter looks at how the search for meaningful measurements of the digital world has evolved over time and how the current thinking about key performance indicators (KPIs) doesn't solve the deeper problems of describing the digital world. Here you look at a framework designed to provide deeper measurement of the digital world: two-tiered segmentation.

Creating a Foundation for Digital Measurement

When I got out of college, I spent a few years working for one of the largest political direct mail companies in the United States. We churned out many millions of pieces during an election cycle. When I first started working there, most of the letters we sent out were preprinted. Every letter was exactly the same, done on a printing press in a continuous roll. We simply ran those rolls through our computer printers. These printed the name and address on the paper where it would show up through the window in the envelope. Machines then stripped away the perforated sides, chopped the letters into nice and even sheets, and stuffed them into the envelopes to be bagged and shipped to the post office and then to your home in mass quantities (sorry about that, too!).

As a programmer, I wrote the code that selected the names to be printed for any given campaign. Not too long after I started, a new piece of technology arrived: the laser printer. These printers weren't your desktop laser printers—they were beasts capable of printing thousands of pages an hour and churning out enough political claptrap to choke every elephant in Africa. But what made them great wasn't that they were faster than the printers we had—they could print every single page differently. Each and every page was computer imaged and could be completely unique, while still looking great and printing at high speed. Now not only could we put somebody's name and address in a fixed location to be shown in a window, but we could actually insert it into the text.

And Gary, we did. Gary, we inserted people's names everywhere. We did it, Gary, because it worked and, Gary, I must admit, we did it because we could. People weren't used to seeing personalized letters from their candidates and they loved it, Gary. Really.

But after a while, Gary, the thrill was gone. People got tired of seeing their name, Gary, especially in places where it didn't really add much. So we stopped doing so much. Gary, I hope you'll agree that's kind of sad.

You're probably wondering why I tell this story.

Well, over the past 15 years, I've built countless digital analytics reports. Over time, those reports have evolved and changed in ways that aren't too dissimilar from my laser printer days.

When we first started building digital reports, we stuffed them with every number we could—and even back then, our tools gave us a lot of numbers. We were generally producing those reports in Excel, and they consisted of a seemingly endless series of tabs, each with its own sizable wall of numbers. And you know what? People loved it. They'd never seen web metrics. You built a website, and you had no idea whether people were using it. So it was pretty cool to see a hits report, a most viewed pages report, and a referring domains report (what's that Google thing?), to get a sense that this digital world was actually real.

But those wall-of-data reports gradually palled. Despite all the data (heck, *because* of all the data), people couldn't find what they needed. The data was too hard to use, too hard to make sense of. People got tired of all that useless data. They wanted less.

And we gave it to them. We gradually began chopping stuff out of the reports. We got KPI fever. KPIs were all we talked about. They were crisp. They were actionable. They were few. We chopped and we chopped until we reduced those walls of data to just one tab, with only a few trend charts and perhaps a dozen KPIs—all nicely colored and boldly fonted, sitting amid lovely little fields of white space.

Those reports looked darn good. People loved them. Really, they did. "This is so clean," they marveled, "so attractive and readable." Those reports didn't have all the clutter; they had just a small number of metrics to look at and act on. Conversion rate is down. Ouch. Visits are up? Excellent. NPS is flat. Oh, well.

But something was still wrong. After a few months of these spare, beautiful little reports, nobody used them anymore. They had palled. It was great at first to know that visits were up, but what exactly did you do with the information? Were visits up because of your SEO program or were you spending money on traffic? Nothing in the KPI gave the answer. Ironically, nothing in the report gave the answer because all the data had been removed.

KPIs without context turned out to be pretty useless. Even worse than this disappointing lack of actionability (and we always talked about KPIs as *actionable* so that the two words went together, like *barren* and *desert* or *texting* and *teens*), KPIs turned out to be a bit misleading and difficult to understand.

When I try to educate executives about digital reporting and KPIs, I show them a slide that has three little case studies based on actual meetings I've had. In the first, the digital analyst announces,

"Our conversion rate has fallen by 5.6 percent in the last two months." Conversion rate (the percentage of visitors to a site who convert— usually to a sale, but also possibly to a lead, a registration, or even an action such as a video view) is the granddaddy of KPIs, the single most common digital key performance indicator. There's silence. Shocked looks. The senior guy in the room looks grim. "It's what I've been saying all along," chimes in the marketing manager. "Our prices are too high—the competition is killing us." The others around the table nod solemnly, for here, it seems, is hard proof in the form of an unimpeachable fall in a key performance indicator. But then the SEO guy, tucked away at the far end of the table, pipes up. "That's not it at all," he says. "We made some major improvements to our long-tail SEO last month, and our page rank on Google has improved considerably for these 400 terms." Here he brandishes a list of keywords provided by his agency. "That means we're getting more traffic to the website. It's probably a bit less qualified, so our conversion rate is down." About half the heads around the table nod in understanding, and everyone goes back to look at their reports. Sadly, those reports have only a small set of KPIs on them, and there's no way to tell which explanation is correct.

Both explanations might be correct—or neither. Countless factors can drive a change in conversion rate on the site. Worse, as our example illustrates, some are good news and some are bad. So not only is it tough for decision makers to tell why a KPI is moving, they can't even decide whether the movement is good or bad.

What's especially telling about this case is that decision makers almost never understand these limitations. Give someone a KPI, and that person will assume that movement in it tracks to an intuitive understanding of good or bad. Conversion rate going up equals good. Conversion rate going down equals bad. Because this isn't correct, giving decision makers these KPIs in isolation is often worse than useless. Quite naturally, they will interpret the movements as good or bad. When you give data to people that leads them to make a bad decision, it doesn't help to suggest that they should have known better. If they should have known better than to naturally interpret the numbers they see, shouldn't the giver have known better than to provide them?

This isn't an isolated example. My second example on the slide uses one of the favorite "soft" metrics at the enterprise level: net promoter score (NPS). NPS is a voice of customer (VoC—sorry about the forest of acronyms here) metric, tracked using online surveys. It measures the percentage of respondents who would recommend your brand. It's widely used largely because of some influential studies suggesting that brand promotion is a stronger predictor of future customer value than measures such as satisfaction. As a KPI, NPS is often used in conjunction with a metric such as conversion rate, and it's designed to capture a softer perspective on success.

Decision makers are right to suspect that it's possible to over-optimize on a single variable. Back in the early days of the Internet, I did quite a bit of work with AOL, the original direct-mail Internet service provider (ISP). If you're too young to remember getting an AOL disk in the mail every week with a "free trial" offer, count your blessings. With its deep background in direct response and reliance on traditional direct response techniques, AOL was a very metrics-driven company—one of the best I've ever worked with.

As dial-up Internet peaked and began to lose subscribers to clearly superior systems, however, that same focus on metrics began to have negative consequences. AOL knew it was leaking subscribers and became very focused on hold rates. To improve those rates, AOL made it impossible to cancel online and trained call operators to do everything possible to discourage cancellations. These tactics worked.

At the time, I felt that AOL was hurting acquisition because it failed to include an online cancellation option. I thought it was eroding its brand. However, the optimization team was able to demonstrate that revenue was maximized by making cancellation very hard indeed.

They were right. Short-term revenue was maximized, and there was no way to prove otherwise because it was true. Given the metrics focus of the company, the cancellation deniers always won.

In one of the first great examples of a social media disaster, a frustrated subscriber recorded a ludicrous phone session in which the agent simply would not process a cancellation. The subscriber posted it online, and it went viral. The effect was disastrous, and the brand (which had already eroded most of its value) collapsed into deep negative equity.

Measuring NPS in conjunction with conversion rate is designed to prevent that type of over-optimization myopia. By having two KPIs that tend to act in opposite directions, decision makers are protected from killing brand equity by too-aggressive drives to conversion or from killing revenue by focusing too much on branding.

Although the intent is sound, presenting NPS in conjunction with conversion rate isn't enough context to create real meaning. Worse, many of the most ardent users of NPS tend to be sites with *no* conversion at all. They become highly myopic on optimizing NPS, in much the same way ecommerce sites often overfocus on conversion rate.

You're probably thinking, that can't be too much of a problem. After all, if you don't have ecommerce on a digital property, can maximizing your brand perception be a bad thing?

Enter example #2. (AOL was just a detour, not the example I had in mind.) A company adopts NPS as its VoC KPI and adds it to the monthly executive dashboard, along with a small number of other critical business measures. Executives tout their customer focus, and managers at every level begin following the metric.

For the first few months, all is well. The metric rises slightly and the organization believes it's well on its way to success. Focusing on the customer is producing measurable improvement. That's what metrics are for.

But then disaster strikes. The company releases a new version of its product, and in the following month, NPS is down significantly. The VoC team presents the bad news to the executive team in the monthly brief. The trend is clear and undeniable. In the aftermath of the new release and upgrade, NPS is truly down.

The knives come out and the blame game starts. Product development, QA, site experience, and marketing folks are all blaming each other for the disastrous rollout. Measurement teams desperately search to find the problem, asking the key question: What don't customers like about the product or the upgrade experience?

The answers are perplexing. The more research they do, the more it seems people prefer the new product to the old—consistently and clearly. What's more, they also prefer the new upgrade experience to the old experience. Better experience, better product, worse NPS.

The executive team gets increasingly frustrated and demands to know what's going on. At last, after countless hours spent chasing down the problem, the answer becomes clear. Nothing is wrong with the new product or the new upgrade experience. Both are clear improvements. NPS is down because, in the wake of an upgrade, the distribution of visit types to the website shifts. A lot more customers come looking for the upgrade, and upgrade visit types tend to be less satisfied customers than new customers.

The following table shows how this works (the numbers are disguised).

	New Visitors %	New Visitors NPS	Upgrader %	Upgrader NPS	Total NPS
Before product upgrade	75%	7.5	25%	6.5	7.25
After product upgrade	55%	7.6	45%	6.7	7.15

NPS went down, even though the ratings for every type of visit went up. What changed? The distribution of visit types. Decision makers are accustomed to consuming data from traditional opinion research techniques, where the sample is carefully isolated from the operations and marketing of the business. With online surveys, that simply isn't the case. Every time you roll out a new marketing campaign or a new product, you subtly shift the sample you're measuring. Ironically, this shifting sample population makes NPS when collected via online intercept surveys one of the most useless and misleading KPIs imaginable. It's almost never measuring what it seems to be measuring, and shifts in it are almost never driven by the obvious interpretation (customer satisfaction is improving or declining). If site-wide NPS derived from online surveys is on your executive dashboard, you should probably fire your measurement team.

Conversion rate and NPS are two of the most common and important KPIs in the digital world, but I suspect that a third will seem absolutely impervious to similar objections: revenue. Revenue has to be good, right? If one KPI must be instantly interpretable, revenue seems like the best candidate. Revenue to business is the equivalent of happiness to utilitarian philosophers; it's the standard currency by which anything can be accurately compared and optimized.

But you know where I'm going with this, right? Not even revenue survives the real-world experience of the absolute uselessness of individual site-wide KPIs. I've got more stories of people misinterpreting revenue numbers than almost any other metric. The AOL example I described earlier is one. That's an extreme example, but two more also show how revenue numbers are commonly misused.

My digital analytics consultancy often works with companies trying to aggressively expand their digital business. Most of these clients are omnichannel, with strong traditional business lines trying to fight off online competitors by providing similar or better online services. When they picked their digital KPIs, it's no surprise that revenue always came out on top. If your goal is to grow your digital business, revenue is a pretty inarguable KPI.

At the end of a successful year working with a brick-and-mortar retailer to build out and improve its digital presence, the company and I put together a terrific executive presentation that highlighted their (and our) successes. They'd scored high double-digit growth in every significant KPI we were measuring: Traffic, conversion rate, and revenue were all up big time. Trifecta!

Unfortunately, a closer look at the business revealed a troubling new perspective on all three of these metrics. In creating online business, we'd targeted the population of customers we had the easiest access to, the company's most loyal and profitable buyers. Using incentives and direct response tactics, we'd been able to drive enough of these folks online to drive that pretty spectacular growth. But detailed analysis of those individual customers suggested that driving them online had not only reduced their profitability, but increased their churn—probably by exposing them to branded ecommerce experiences that weren't yet as good as their best online competition's. In short, we'd damaged the core audience of the business and reduced profitability, even while driving double-digit revenue gains. Pat us on the back.

In omnichannel companies, this type of siloed revenue optimization at the expense of the business is extremely common and is only encouraged by a wrong-headed focus on site KPIs such as revenue. Now consider an example we had nothing to do with, but that I think is one of the funniest and most telling I've ever heard.

A large financial services company had a pretty big auto insurance business. Like most such businesses, it had started offline, but digital commerce had become a significant part of its total business—auto insurance is one of the easiest insurance products to sell digitally. The digital business was measured separately and had its own completely siloed KPIs. When auto policies came up for renewal, the company's offline arm traditionally sent out a mailer with an easy renewal notice. People being what they are, this nearly always worked and the renewal rates were quite high. What's more, renewals were by far the most profitable part of the business because renewals weren't price shopping in the brutally competitive online space. New policies issued to customers online were almost always significantly cheaper (and less profitable) than if the customer simply opted for an offline automatic renewal.

But for an online team measured and incented on revenue, those highly brand-loyal and sure-to-convert renewers were just too tempting an audience to resist. The team targeted a digital campaign to those customers, bringing them to the website for a quote renewal experience that nearly always resulted in a cheaper-for-the-customer and less-profitable-for-the-company policy.

This is almost the reverse of the AOL case and, to me, it's less clear that a mistake is being made. In the long run, giving your loyal customers the same (or better) deal that you give new customers is good business. But what's funny about this example is that the C-suite had no idea this was happening, yet it was certainly damaging the short-term bottom-line. Instead, the company focused on a siloed KPI that just happened to be revenue. And the team taking advantage of that was far less concerned with the state of the customer than with its own performance goals. I've always suspected that if the C-suite had understood what was happening, it wouldn't have been pleased.

Doing the right thing out of ignorance is no way to run a business.

The bottom line is simple and straightforward. No matter how important, thoughtful, or business driven KPIs are, they are inherently flawed when used as a way to understand the digital world. They misrepresent reality, underdetermine action, and lack sufficient context to drive understanding. Our multi-year drive to simplify the data we provided and make it more business driven was a failure.

In retrospect, this really shouldn't have surprised us. When you think about measuring the world, how often does a single metric (or even a small set of metrics) provide sufficient information to understand a situation and act? Imagine driving a car with one piece of information. It's no knock on speed as a driving KPI to suggest that, if it's the only data point you have when driving, your chances of getting where you need to go alive are minimal. Why should it differ for a complex digital business with tens of thousands of content assets, millions of different and unique visitors, and hundreds of marketing and site initiatives all happening simultaneously?

So where do we start?

Two-Tiered Segmentation

Oddly, the best place to start when it comes to measuring digital worlds is with people. People are actually far more fundamental to the digital world than to the physical world. We can conceive of the physical world without people. A huge, beautiful, complex universe could well exist devoid of people and mind, a universe with mass, velocity, and hundreds of other properties. That makes no sense in the digital world. At the deepest level of artificial reality, what matters most are people.

It's true for your digital properties as well. The first and most basic question about your digital world is, who uses it? If you walk into my office and announce that visitors to our website are up by 5,000 this month, my first question isn't about what pages they viewed, or how long they spent on the site, or what campaigns drove them here. None of that stuff matters unless and until I understand who *they* are. Were those visitors customers? Prospects? Job seekers? Stock pickers? Weird netizens who accidentally clicked on the display ad we popped up on their favorite mobile website? It makes all the difference in the world.

Most conversation on digital measurement and performance assumes that the overwhelming majority of visits and behavior on our digital properties are exactly what we expect: customers and prospects doing the types of things the site is built for. Sometimes that's true. But a surprising amount of the time, it isn't. I've measured websites on which one in five visitors is a job seeker. That's hell on your conversion rates, but they sure make your content look engaging. Job seekers can and do read anything and everything on your website. I've seen display campaigns in which 99 percent of the click-throughs were accidental. I've seen acquisition websites on which a flat-out majority of the visitors are customers trying to find a phone number to call.

These situations arise precisely because the digital world is invisible. In a store, we'd realize it if most people who came in the door immediately turned around and left, asked for a job application, or were carrying a return. On the web, we don't generally see this. And part of the reason we don't is the fault of those metrics on page views, time onsite, visits, and so on—they don't help much in figuring out who our visitors are.

How do you answer that "who" question? The answer has two parts. The first part is traditional visitor segmentation. For example, we might answer the "who" question with a list of names: Gary, Janice, Donna, Karen, and so on. But that isn't the type of answer we're looking for (unless we know all the people who use our digital property). We're really looking for a way to understand the relationship we have with our digital users. Are they customers or prospects? Are they high value or low value? Are they brand enthusiasts or detractors? Are they married with children or just out of college? That's segmentation.

Businesses have been segmenting their customers for a long time. Segmentations divide people into interestingly differentiated groups. Every business has segments, and for every business, they are potentially infinite and unique. There's no one right segmentation and there's no single right way to create a segmentation, but segmentation is always useful. I've never studied a digital property that can't be or shouldn't be segmented.

For some digital properties, we can fully and exhaustively answer the "who" question. If you log into a banking or brokerage site, a medical services site, or an online services site, all the information known about you can be attached to the digital behavior. When you log in, a bank knows you're a customer. It knows which products you own. It knows your account balance. It knows your age, your social security number, and your occupation. It knows how much money you have in your account and how long you've been a customer. The bank probably knows whether you have kids and what age they are. It knows a heck of a lot. And banks use this information all the time (although not always in digital measurement) to help them understand what offers you might be interested in and how they should market to you. All that stuff is part of their segmentation. Indeed, banks know so much about their customers that they have to create mathematical models to reduce all those data points into a simpler, easier-to-use method of segmentation.

Many digital properties don't know their people, but that doesn't mean they aren't using segmentation. At a minimum, every website tracks whether it recognizes a visitor from a previous visit. It tracks the visitor location (at about the city level) you're connecting from. It recognizes what device you're using, what browser, and what type of connection. It knows what time of day and what day of the week you're visiting on. That's all pretty thin gruel, and it's a far cry from knowing how much money you have in your checking and savings accounts. It's still the basis for a segmentation. And many a "who" question in the digital world is answered with some combination of these bare facts. In Chapter 4, "Customer Identity and Taxonomy," I describe better ways to answer the "who" question than using these bare-bones data points. For now, I'll just say that, however thin the answer to the "who" question is, it's the starting point to understanding the digital world.

That this is just the starting point should be obvious.

When we know who the visitors to our website are, we have the initial kernel of understanding about the digital world. Those 5,000 new visitors? Customers.

That's potentially interesting, but it isn't enough. Were those customers here to buy more products? Were they trying to complain about the service they've received? Were they looking for a phone number or the location of a branch or office? It makes a huge difference.

If the first question we need to understand about digital is "who," the second question is "what"—what was a visitor trying to accomplish?

If we could understand who used a digital property and what they were trying to accomplish, we'd have a fantastically better understanding of a particular digital world. We'd find it much easier, for example, to decide whether our digital property is successful. We'd even find it easier to decide whether our website is successful for each type of visitor and visit.

A fundamental and important fact about the digital world is that the success of your digital property is relative to your visitors' intent. Your goals won't always be identical to your visitors'. Nobody comes to a website looking to be upsold, but for almost every commerce site, upselling visitors is a legitimate business goal. So your goals might not be identical, but your desire to upsell a customer and your ability to do it is bound up with visit intent. If a visitor came to complain about a product, your chance of upselling them is pretty much zero.

Unless your digital property has only one type of visitor and one type of visit, the way you measure success will never be singular. A classic example involves the metric of time onsite. Is it good when a visitor spends more time on your site? In the early days of web analytics, we always assumed that the answer to that question was yes.

Unfortunately, plenty of evidence points to the contrary. Time onsite doesn't correlate particularly well to other key site outcomes. What's more, when some of the longest sessions are studied individually, they look like absolute failures. When determined visitors can't find what they're looking for on a digital property, they can consume a lot of content and spend a lot of time looking around. That time isn't making them happy, though—the more time they spend, the worse they feel about the experience. Nobody ever suggested that the longer a customer spends in the call center, the better off everyone is!

So is spending more time on a website always bad? Of course not. If visitors spend that time perusing engaging content, chances are good that the more time they spent, the happier they are, the better their experience was, and the more valuable the visit was. It's the same metric, but with two fundamentally different interpretations, depending on what the visitor was trying to do.

It goes back to that disastrous simplifying assumption that the main purpose of a digital property is the only purpose of the digital property and that the most common type of visitor and visit is the *only* type of visitor and visit.

If you know who the visitors to your digital property are and what they are trying to accomplish, you have a framework for easily answering more questions. Were visitors successful? What metrics are best for measuring that success? Did a change work? Those questions all become far more comprehensible.

I have a name for this framework that helps you understand who visitors in a digital space are and what they are trying to accomplish: two-tiered segmentation. The first tier is the *who*, the traditional segmentation of visitors by business-significant dimensions. The second tier is the uniquely digital tier, the *what*. It's a segmentation based on what visitors are trying to accomplish.

Two-tiered segmentation is critical for truly understanding the digital world. But so far, it's just a framework. Now it's time to look at how you can use the digital measurements you collect to instantiate this framework.

Signal to Noise: Another View on Two-Tiered Segmentation

One way that analysts talk about data is signal and noise. When you analyze data, you're looking for a signal, a pattern or relationship in the data that is significant or important. This task is hard because nearly every real data set has a lot of noise. That noise might be random variation, or uninteresting or secondary relationships might cause patterns to emerge. Statisticians have ways of testing data to see how likely it is that a pattern is generated randomly. But no statistical test in the world can identify the difference between interesting signals in the data—signals driven by real causal relationships—and signals driven by uninteresting relationships. For example, there's a strong relationship between owning a Mercedes and being wealthy. That doesn't mean buying a Mercedes will make you wealthy—quite the reverse. The relationship exists because of the fact that Mercedes is generally an expensive car brand. This signal might be useful if we know what cars people own and we want to predict their wealth. If we want to understand how people become wealthy, the correlation between owning a Mercedes and having wealth is just noise.

You can usefully think of two-tiered segmentation as a way to amplify the signal and reduce the noise from web metrics. Consider an example from a hospitality company that shaped some of the original thinking around two-tiered segmentation. Similar to most companies at the time, this hotel chain focused on look-to-book rates as the most important digital KPI. Look-to-book is a simple and undeniably important metric. It's the number of bookings relative to the number of shoppers—in this case, visits to the website. As the single most important digital metric, it had extraordinary visibility at every level in the company, right up to the C-suite.

Suddenly, in one night, the look-to-book rate tanked. And it stayed down. When your most significant KPI tanks, it tends to set off alarm bells. When that KPI has C-suite visibility, the alarm bells are loud. After much panic and thrashing, the explanation emerged. The company had rolled out a change in the way its on-property Wi-Fi worked. When visitors logged into the Wi-Fi, they were deposited on the main home page of the website, the same website used by people booking a room. Naturally, visits went up. Bookings didn't. The result was a sharp decline in look-to-book, their primary KPI.

It's disturbing that an essentially meaningless change in the way the business works can trigger a huge change in a fundamental business performance indicator. It should create doubt. How many other unrelated factors live inside of and influence the look-to-book rate but have nothing to do with actual conversion effectiveness? When we started thinking this way, it became obvious that a significant percentage of all site visits were unrelated to booking a room. When we looked at it in detail, we saw clear evidence of this. We got the same result when we simply asked people with an online survey. People came to the site to find the address or phone number for a specific property, to see whether the property they'd already booked had a pool, to look for a job, to change their email address in the rewards program, and, robotically, to check out a competitor's price. Probably the largest single percentage of visitors who weren't actually shopping were those looking for information about a specific property they'd already booked. The chances of selling these people another room? Zero.

On this particular site, the number of people looking for a job was a fairly small but not insignificant percentage. However, on some sites we've measured, job seekers have turned out to be as much as a quarter of all site users. A Big Four consulting company will have many thousands of visitors every week who are looking for a job. That's not a bad thing. Recruitment is a key function for an enterprise website in the consulting business. But those people aren't going to generate leads. If you're measuring the ratio of leads to visits, most of what you're then measuring is seasonal fluctuations in the job market.

What's particularly amusing about job seekers is that they don't just look at the careers page on a website. That would be too boring. If we track people who do look at the careers page, we almost always see that they are heavy consumers of every section of the website. Between curiosity and interview prep, they spend time and view content everywhere. They tend to look very much like your most engaged customers—but they never seem to convert. I suppose it's not impossible to sell a job seeker something, but if variation in the number of job seekers is driving changes in your conversion rate, that isn't helpful to running your business.

Nothing is wrong with using conversion rate or look-to-book as metrics. They are legitimately interesting measures of performance in the digital world. But they're interesting only after you've narrowed the universe of their application to the visits and visitors for whom they are appropriate. Site-wide KPIs just aren't useful.

Every data set has a certain amount of random variation that makes it harder to detect real patterns. Being random, this variation can go in all directions—and at times, this variation can look very non-random indeed. Most of the examples I've given are cases in which eliminating the noise in the data helped hone in on the real signal (the KPI). In our look-to-book example, noise is generated by every visitor who comes to the website and isn't shopping for a room. By eliminating those people, we can track a good signal around look-to-book.

I've chosen to frame the discussion on KPIs and metrics primarily around segmentation, not signal to noise. Two-tiered segmentation provides a real framework for thinking about the digital world, which signal to noise doesn't do. Nothing is wrong (and, actually, much is right) with the idea that you want to minimize noise in the system to effectively measure the underlying signal. As an approach, however, it doesn't provide much guidance on how to do it in the digital realm. Two-tiered segmentation does provide that guidance. By separating out every distinct type of visit, it eliminates the single largest source of noise in digital measurement across a huge range of problems.

Understanding Two-Tiered Segmentations

The easiest way to think of this two-tiered segmentation is as a matrix. Start with your audience, the *who*. Then layer in the *why*, the types of visits people make to your digital properties.

How does this actually look? The easiest way to visualize it is with some real-world examples. Before we go there, though, it's important to point out that although this two-tiered segmentation is meant to be a general-purpose conceptual model, the actual instantiation of it is custom to every digital property. It's not meant to be a general-purpose scheme that you often find described as the purchase funnel (see Figure 2.1).

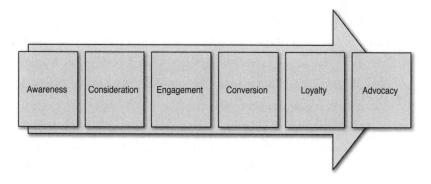

Figure 2.1 An engagement life-cycle

These types of models have their utility, but if you think about the earlier examples, it's pretty obvious that stage-based visitor classification won't solve most of the problems described. When an on-property hotel visitor logs into the Wi-Fi and accesses the home page, what stage is that visitor at? What's more, this type of model conflates every type of visitor at a single stage. That's just not right. When I ask who comes to our website, I want to know more about them than their consideration stage. Finally, this type of life-stage model is interesting for a fairly wide range of ecommerce and lead-generation sites, but does it feel useful for a customer support site, a content-based publishing site, a social network site, or a government site? Not really.

So in creating a certain enterprise-specific two-tiered segmentation, it's best to throw out other people's models and think carefully about your business. For the first part of the two-tiered segmentation (the who), you can often start with the type of persona-based visitor segmentation or relationship categorization people have been using to drive marketing programs for many, many years.

Keep in mind, however, that this type of categorization won't exhaust the full range of visitors who actually come to your digital properties. In your traditional relationship-/persona-based segmentations, there's an implicit assumption that the pool contains only a self-selected set of actual or potential customers. On digital properties, that isn't usually the case. Job seekers, journalists, employees, robotic price checkers, investors, students, and accidental clickers (people with fat fingers like me who accidentally click on your mobile ad while trying to close it) might all find reasons to visit your website. You don't necessarily need to care about them, and it's not unusual to dump all or most of these into an "other" bucket. Sometimes these visitors do matter, though. For example, you might be interested in how your employees use your website. If you're a startup, investors might be the single most important group of visitors you have. And as we've already mentioned, job seekers are a distinct and potentially valuable segment of your audience to understand and optimize. In most cases, however, these groups are important largely in the negative sense—you want to eliminate them from the other segments so they aren't creating noise in the analysis.

If the first tier of the segmentation (visitor type) *should* be customized to the enterprise, the second tier (visit type) *must* be customized. The reason or intent behind a visit to the digital property is the driving force when it comes to the actual behavior exhibited.

When you think about this second tier, stay firmly focused on the customer's intent. You don't want to define visit types in terms of channel source, tool used, or business goals. Customers didn't come to your website because they wanted to click on a pay-per-click ad. That's how they chose to get there. It may be a significant fact, but it isn't a visit type. Similarly, customers didn't come to your website to use your search functionality. That may be what they do first, but they search because they're looking for something to read or buy. Again, the tools visitors use are often significant, but they are never a visit intent.

Finally, don't confuse your goals with your visitors' intent. People don't come to your website to be upsold. That might be your business goal for a specific type of visit, but it's never a visit intent. People come to a website to be entertained, research a product, compare prices, buy a specific product, find information to help solve a customer support problem, find your nearest store, lodge a complaint, register their warranty, and so on. Those visit intents set the table for their actual behavior and form the basis of the second tier of segmentation. If you always reflect back on a visit type with this customer intent lens, you won't go wrong when it comes to thinking about visit types.

Sample Two-Tiered Segmentations

In the following list, you'll find some high-level two-tiered segmentations for different industries. This isn't meant to be comprehensive, and in pretty much every case, the segmentations are considerably simplified. They should give you a pretty good sense of how a digital segmentation might look and how they are specific to every business/digital world.

- Figure 2.2 is a sample I use all the time, originally derived from an investment services/brokerage site. The first-tier segmentation is a classic customer parsing of advisors and managers or investors. Advisors might be doing fund research just like investors, but the success metrics are different. The main point is that success metrics live inside the matrix of who a visitor is and what that person is trying to accomplish.

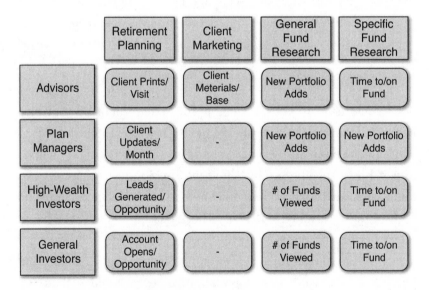

	Retirement Planning	Client Marketing	General Fund Research	Specific Fund Research
Advisors	Client Prints/ Visit	Client Meterials/ Base	New Portfolio Adds	Time to/on Fund
Plan Managers	Client Updates/ Month	-	New Portfolio Adds	New Portfolio Adds
High-Wealth Investors	Leads Generated/ Opportunity	-	# of Funds Viewed	Time to/on Fund
General Investors	Account Opens/ Opportunity	-	# of Funds Viewed	Time to/on Fund

Figure 2.2 Brokerage segmentation

- If you're running a content site, the traditional business-focused segmentation with investing might make you wonder whether the same segmentation concepts apply. They do. Figure 2.3 is an example from a pure-play, mostly anonymous publishing site. The *who* segmentation focuses on how the user tends to access content. The *what* segmentation captures the intent. Was the user doing a start- or end-of-day news check, looking for something local, or trying to find something specific?

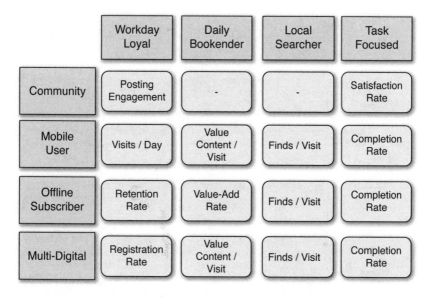

	Workday Loyal	Daily Bookender	Local Searcher	Task Focused
Community	Posting Engagement	-	-	Satisfaction Rate
Mobile User	Visits / Day	Value Content / Visit	Finds / Visit	Completion Rate
Offline Subscriber	Retention Rate	Value-Add Rate	Finds / Visit	Completion Rate
Multi-Digital	Registration Rate	Value Content / Visit	Finds / Visit	Completion Rate

Figure 2.3 Content segmentation

- We've built these types of segmentation frameworks for almost every kind of digital property. Figure 2.4 shows a simplified example from a social-focused campaign that was trying to get teams to enroll in a competition and then vote on different projects. The *who* segmentation captures a pretty classic engagement life stage. The visit type is all about why visitors were doing something. Note how the success metrics in this process were often relative to users moving into new visit types of categories.

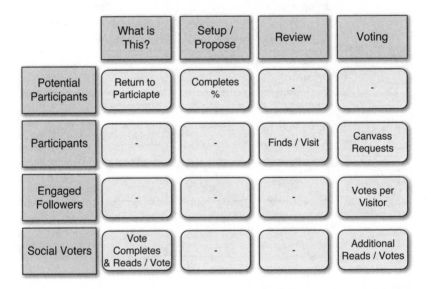

Figure 2.4 Social segmentation

- Figure 2.5 shows an example from a manufacturing site with a branding focus. The audience types (who) ranged from consumers, to developers, to resellers. We identified these populations by a combination of registration and key content usage. The visit types (what) reflected a range of activities that responded to the many different types of content they deployed. Success metrics in this case varied mostly by visit type, but they weren't all that different by type of visitor.

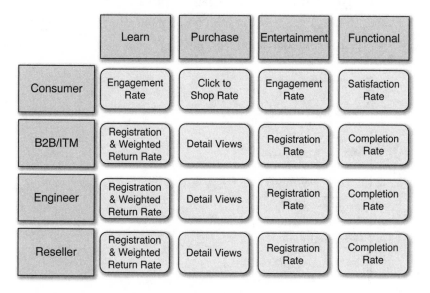

	Learn	Purchase	Entertainment	Functional
Consumer	Engagement Rate	Click to Shop Rate	Engagement Rate	Satisfaction Rate
B2B/ITM	Registration & Weighted Return Rate	Detail Views	Registration Rate	Completion Rate
Engineer	Registration & Weighted Return Rate	Detail Views	Registration Rate	Completion Rate
Reseller	Registration & Weighted Return Rate	Detail Views	Registration Rate	Completion Rate

Figure 2.5 Manufacturing segmentation

- Figure 2.6 illustrates a different slant on visitor segmentation in the digital world. This bank had a rich and powerful customer segmentation, but it wanted to understand how visitors used online banking. The visit dimension captured specific transaction types, but the bank wanted to create a visitor-based behavioral segmentation to live underneath its traditional segments. We looked at the overall patterns in the way users used the online bank application. These patterns not only helped us understand who is most engaged with the OLB application, but they also made it easier to understand which patterns were optimal, profitable, and satisfying.

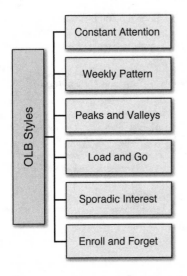

Figure 2.6 OLB segmentation

- The customer support segmentation in Figure 2.7 is a close corollary to the earlier OLB segmentation. For many multichannel customer support models, the most important information to know about customers is how they like to receive service. You can use demographics, but a behavioral answer is far more accurate. This segmentation tracked transaction journeys by type, to identify customers who prefer digital or call servicing, by difficulty of transaction. This type of segmentation is great for targeting service messages and for understanding when digital or call functionality is failing.

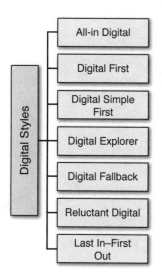

Figure 2.7 Digital style segmentation

Effectively measuring the digital world begins (and I say this without a hint of irony) with understanding people. Always, always, always ask who your audience is and what those people are trying to accomplish. Their agenda sets the table for your success. And unless and until you've framed your measurement so that your KPIs are specific to the visitors and visit types on your digital properties, your KPIs and metrics are only measuring noise.

3

Use Cases and Visit Intent

Two-tiered segmentation sounds great. I'd sure love to know who my visitors are and what they're trying to accomplish. In the digital world, though, visitors are mostly or entirely anonymous. I see a vapor trail in the sky, but I never see the airplane and I never get to talk to the pilot. So how can I possibly understand visitor intent, or what visitors are trying to accomplish? This is the single most important problem in understanding the digital world. The solution to this problem gives us a proven path to solving many other problems in digital measurement.

Few people fail to see the immediate appeal and deep power of measuring the digital world using a combination of visitor and visit intent segmentation. Knowing who visitors are and what they are trying to accomplish is obviously superior to measuring artifacts such as page views. But those who open a digital analytics tool will search in vain for a report that captures this type of segmentation. And those who understand the actual data that is collected will rightly ask how it's possible, in the largely anonymous world of digital, to capture either of these foundational elements. Except for certain "logged-in" properties, we don't know who our visitors are, and we most certainly don't know what they are trying to accomplish.

This second tier of segmentation, what visitors are trying to accomplish, is the more fundamental of the two tiers. Not only is it unique to digital, but it is richer in affect. Far more than visitor type, visit intent tends to dominate our view of what happened in the digital world and determine whether that experience was a success.

One of the great fallacies that plagues us when we interpret the physical world around us is to read intention into nature. When popularizers of bad biology argue for survival of the fittest, they add a subtle layer of intention to a process that has none. If by "fittest" we substitute the phrase "most likely to survive," we have a closer understanding of the near-tautology that is evolutionary theory. Those that are most likely to survive are...the most likely to survive. Not *guaranteed* to survive. Not *chosen* or *selected*. Just *more likely* to survive. What makes evolution more than a simple and stupid tautology is the mechanism of mutation coupled with inheritance that turns "more likely to survive" into something interesting. Nature doesn't care whether your genes survive. Your genes don't care whether they survive. Genes don't have intentions, nor does nature.

We bake intentions into all sorts of activities that are merely random or statistical. We talk about players "getting hot," despite all the evidence to the contrary. We knock on wood when we mention how light the traffic is. We read our horoscopes in the paper. It's all absurd. The world doesn't have intention or purpose.

Here's where things get interesting. The digital world has intention baked in. Unlike our natural world, it's built with intention. People don't randomly construct a website. They don't select content to assemble by rolling a giant pair of Google dice.

Unlike the natural world, the digital world is built by us. It's a construction of code, images, and content that we've erected for a specific purpose. This gives us a huge advantage when we try to understand what people are doing in the digital world.

Angel's Taco Divina Food Trucks: Designing a Digital Segmentation

We return to this idea of intention repeatedly as we build out a complete foundation for digital measurement. Let's say you're the proud owner of six of the finest taco stands in greater Los Angeles. Plenty of people love your tacos, but they can't always find your mobile stands. And, of course, not everybody knows how great your tacos are. Some people out there still don't believe you can get great food at a mobile taco stand. You're also thinking about adding a seventh stand, and you'll need a crack team of taco chefs to support that new stand.

So you build a website. The main page introduces Angel's Taco Divina (ATD) mobile stands. It contains a big picture of your taco stands, some text that describes your heavenly carnitas, and links to three different pages. One of those pages shows the current location of every mobile stand. The second page details all the great reviews ATD has gotten from discerning standies. The last page touts great opportunities for new employees to master the culinary art of the carnitas taco and earn their black belt in tacology.

Each page of the Angel's Taco Divina website was built for a specific purpose and with intention. We can use that knowledge to help understand our visitors. When visitors land on the home page of ATD, we're not really sure why they are there. Did they land by mistake, are they looking to find a truck, did they hear something about ATD and want to know more, or are they looking for a job? There's no way to know.

Until they click.

When they choose a link on the home page, we suddenly have a much better idea of why they are there. It's important, though, to understand the limitations of what we know. Maybe a visitor arrived on the website because he or she wants to buy ATD, lock stock and barrel—not a taco, but the whole enchilada. The original website isn't built to serve that kind of buyer. No link reads, Click Here If You

Want to Buy Angel's Taco Divina. Maybe the potential buyer chooses a link. Maybe not. Either way, that click isn't going to tell us that we have a potential buyer.

There's a simple but important lesson here. Using our design intentions to understand what visitors are trying to accomplish works only when the content we build happens to match what visitors want to do. So it's not perfect, but it is something.

For now, we're going to assume that our design matches most visitors' intentions. As great as ATD is, we don't have a flood of potential buyers out there. We have ways to check this, but that's a topic for later. For right now, it's good enough to assume that most of the people who click the Find a Truck link actually want to find a taco truck.

If we think this way, then we can postulate that ATD's website has four types of use cases. We have visitors who come to find a truck, visitors who come to find out more about ATD because they might want to try a taco, and visitors who come looking for a job. Then we have people who come for any other reason but who won't find any content to satisfy them. That's it.

What's more, we can build a set of rules that use visitors' behavior to classify them by intent. Here's a sample of the rules.

Behavior	Use Case
Lands on home page and clicks on Find a Truck OR lands on Find a Truck and exits	Find a Truck
Lands on home page and clicks on More About Our Tacos OR lands on MAOT and exits	Try a Taco
Lands on home page and clicks on Jobs OR lands on Jobs and exits	Job Seeker
Lands on home page and exits	Other

We might have a fairly high degree of confidence that these rules capture something valid and that, with them, we can classify the four types of visits to our site and use them to understand how frequent each type of visit is. But a moment's reflection (or less) should make it obvious that we've captured only a subset of the possible patterns on the website. For example, our rules haven't captured some other patterns:

> Lands on home page
>> Clicks on Jobs
>> Clicks on home page
>> Clicks on More About Our Tacos
>
> Lands on Find a Truck
>> Clicks on home page
>> Clicks on More About Our Tacos
>
> Lands on More About Our Tacos
>> Clicks on Find a Truck

In each of these cases, we have a more complex set of behaviors that combine elements of each of the original use cases. In the first case, the visitor landed on the home page and then clicked through to the Jobs page. After returning to the home page, the visitor clicked More About Our Tacos. So is this someone looking for a job or someone interested in trying a taco?

Either could be true—or both interpretations might be incorrect. In this case, we can likely assume that the visitor's first action, looking at the Jobs page, is the initial intent. Someone who wants to try a taco is much less likely to be interested in a job than the reverse. What's more, a good job seeker is quite likely to check out the More About Our Tacos page, in case it comes up in an interview, or just to decide whether we're the kind of company worth committing time to. So job seeking is a dominant action over taco trying.

In this case, we have two reasons for thinking that we should classify the first pattern as a job seeker, not a taco tryer: first click and dominant interest. Of course, we can make this case even more complex by looking at a chain of behaviors, like this:

Lands on home page

Clicks on More About Our Tacos

Clicks on home page

Clicks on Jobs

Now the first click is More About Our Tacos and the second click is Jobs. What should we think when our two cues conflict? In this case, I'd be inclined to think that Jobs still triumphs. Jobs is so dominant a behavior that it trumps first click.

What about our second case:

Lands on Find a Truck, then clicks on home page and clicks on More About Our Tacos

This is a trickier case. There's no reason to think that Find a Truck or More About Our Tacos is a dominant behavior. People could come for either—and they might well come for both. It's also possible that landing on Find a Truck was accidental. The visitor might have been searching for information about ATD, but Google might have surfaced the Find a Truck page as the most popular link.

We don't have one right answer here. Given this pattern of behavior, some visitors likely were primarily focused on finding a truck but were curious about our tacos, some were equally interested, and some were primarily focused on our tacos but happened to land on Find a Truck. Don't fall into the trap of certainty. But are we stuck? If so, how can we describe the visitors with this pattern?

We aren't stuck yet.

Digital behavior (at least, what we track) is surprisingly simple but richer than it first appears. If we're trying to figure out whether a visitor is more interested in finding a truck or learning more about tacos, we can look at a few other behaviors. Let's start with that entry on Find a Truck. Visitors don't just arrive on a website. They either enter your URL directly, have your page bookmarked, click through from a link (on an ad, post, video, tweet, site, and so on), or click through from a search. All this information is stored in a field called the referring site. It tells you the URL (if known) the user came from.

If that field is empty, it means the user came directly to your page. A direct land on Find a Truck means your user has been there before. That user has either directly bookmarked the page or typed in the URL. Either way, that user isn't new to ATD. So the click on More About Our Tacos is probably intentional. But what about the land on Find a Truck?

Did the visitor just have the page bookmarked as the most convenient place of entry, yet the visit was all about reading more about tacos? Or was the visit about finding a truck and then, as an addition, reading even more about tacos? To help answer that question, we can look at a metric called time on page. Time on page is one of the trickiest and most misused metrics in digital analytics. Its technical definition is a bit complex, but in general, it's the measured time between two page requests on your website by the same visitor. Using it as a general measure is tricky, but in this case, it can be illuminating. If our visitor wanted to read about tacos and didn't care about the location of our trucks, chances are good that the time spent on Find a Truck is minimal and probably much less than in previous visits.

We can then write our use case rules like this:

Lands on Find a Truck then clicks on home page and clicks on More About Our Tacos

If (Land on Find a Truck and clicks on home page and clicks on More About Our Tacos) AND

(Entry on Find a Truck is direct) AND

(Time on Find a Truck < 20 seconds) THEN use case is Interested in Tacos

Most digital analytics tools support segmentations like this. However, not every segmentation strategy can be instantiated in every tool. Some strategies are challenging to implement unless you are working with raw data in an analytics warehouse. For example, if the segmentation rule used variations in this visitor's time on page, it would be much harder to implement in a traditional digital analytics solution:

> If (Land on Find a Truck and clicks on home page and clicks on More About Our Tacos) AND
>
> (Entry on Find a Truck is direct) AND
>
> (Time on Find a Truck this visit) < .5 * AVG (previous time on page) THEN use case is Interested in Tacos

Obviously, this kind of exercise can get fairly complex. ATD is an absurdly simple site, but even so, we could spend a lot of time generating rules to cover every type of behavioral pattern. We can learn two lessons from this: First, digital analytics isn't easy. Second, no completely "correct" answer can identify all the use cases on any website.

Building Segmentation Rules

The behaviors that uniquely identify a use case are a kind of behavioral signature. The segmentation rules are just a formal description of that signature. Translating these descriptions into code in a digital analytics solution or analytics warehouse provides a means of classifying each actual visit to the website by use case or intent.

When you first build a segmentation rule, it's important to check and validate the behaviors you've singled out. This validation is an important step, and not just because it's easy to miscode segmentation logic. It's not uncommon to find that even when the logic you've built is correct by your original definition, the resulting segment doesn't quite capture the behavior you thought or is problematic in some other way.

Keep in mind that the purpose of a segmentation is to achieve a relatively homogenous population in purpose, likelihood of success, and content consumption. If it fails in any of these respects, it might be flawed when used for reporting, testing, or personalization.

The next sections look at common segmentation issues.

The Segment Is Too Small

No ready-made definition identifies what "too small" means when it comes to segmentation. In the example I gave earlier, we might have no nonzero segment of potential acquirers for ATD that is too small to be of interest. However, if almost no one goes directly to the More About Our Tacos page, it might not be worth keeping that use case. A too-small segment is simply one that isn't of current interest, because the behavior is either extremely uncommon, inherently not very interesting or valuable, or simply not a business priority.

The Segment Is Too Large

Picky, aren't we? But just as a segment that doesn't pick out enough behavior is a problem, it's also a concern if too many people belong to a segment. Imagine that every visitor fell within one segment (for instance, a segment defined as viewing at least one page). Just as a difference that makes no difference is no difference, a segmentation that doesn't segment isn't a segmentation. Many digital properties could identify a large, undifferentiated segment of visitors with little or no interesting behavior. Landing on the home page and then exiting is a common example. You can't do much about this. But if you have a segment of potential buyers that represents more than half your visitors, maybe you should look for ways to divide that segment more finely.

For example, it's often useful to classify a use case not just by what the visitors are trying to accomplish, but also by where they are in their journey and how prepared or committed they are to the journey. This isn't division for division's sake. When you have populations inside a segment that are distinct in terms of the kind of content they consume or in their likelihood of success, it's important to split them apart wherever possible. This last point about success is particularly interesting and important. When first defining use cases, many analysts mistakenly take a site-based view of a potential use case. It's not uncommon for an analyst to create use cases out of actions such as "using internal search." Now, users of internal search are sometimes a distinct population on a site, but they are almost never an appropriate use case. The whole point of this type of segmentation is to move from an asset-based view of the digital world to a people-based view. The ATD case shows how fine a line this can be. For ATD, we took something like viewing the Find a Truck page and made it equivalent to a use case called Looking for Taco Stands. By shifting from a page view to a visit intent, questions like these become far more comprehensible: Were visitors successful? What metrics are best for measuring that success? Did a change work? So it's easy to see how an analyst might take something such as an internal search and create a use case called Using Internal Search. But the two are not equivalent. In the first, what we know about the content describes the user's intent. That simply isn't the case with internal search. People didn't come to the website to "Use Internal Search." In fact, internal search typically represents many use cases that depend on what the user searches for.

That being said, a use case can and often does embody more than just a visitor's intent. Imagine that Visitor A arrives at a site intending to buy a BitBuster 2000X Model 3. Visitor B arrives at the same site wanting to see whether the BitBuster 2000X is cheaper or more expensive than the competitor's ByteBanger 800Z. Visitor C arrives at the site looking to investigate important features. All three visitors can reasonably be described as being in a shopping use case. However, given sufficient content, we can expect each of these visitors to take a different route, we'd measure our success differently (at least, in the short run), and we'd expect to have different success rates for each. Splitting these visitors into a Ready to Buy, Price Shopping, and Features Researching set of use cases will yield more interesting results and more actionable segmentations. So how do you know when to stop splitting a segment? As with the process of defining a segment, you don't have a sure-fire answer. It's not uncommon to get to a point at which you think finer segmentations might exist, but your content simply doesn't support splitting them out. In other cases, you might lack the business resources to effectively use any of the differences between two subsegments. In creating a segmentation, you always face a trade-off between accuracy and simplicity, and each has value.

The Segment Conflates Two Use Cases

As should be fairly obvious from the preceding discussion, every segment that contains more than one visitor probably conflates two use cases if you push the grounds for segmentation to the extreme. That isn't troubling on its own, but sometimes the behavioral signature for a use case captures two completely different types of activity. Most hotel and travel sites have a good example of this. Let's say you want to book a hotel for your trip to New York City in a month. You're a loyal traveler, so you ignore the Online Travel Agents (OTAs) and go directly to the website of your favorite property chain. You search on New York City and get a list of hotels. You click one that's close to your meeting place and check it out. If it looks good, you click the Book Now button and reserve a room.

Now imagine that you return to that website three weeks later because you want to find the phone number of the hotel where you'll be staying. You go directly to the website and search on New York City to get a list of hotels. You click the property where you're staying and look up the hotel phone number. Then you leave.

These two sessions create identical behavior trails, right up to the point of success (see Figure 3.1).

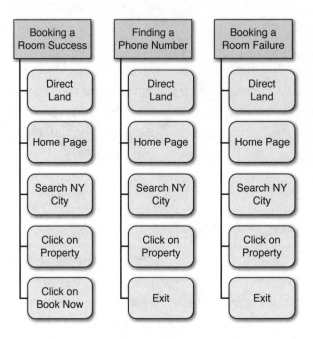

Figure 3.1 Identical behaviors and very different user intents

You can't differentiate between the shopping and phone number use cases by adding the Book Now click to your behavioral signature. That's a disaster. Every shopping session would be a success! But if your behavioral signature is limited to something like Searched and Clicked on a Property Detail, you can be almost certain that your use case has conflated these two separate activities.

As with most complex activities, there are likely to be an infinitude of ways to go wrong. At a high level, the best way to judge a segmentation is by the degree to which it's fit for the purpose. A segmentation has to segment; the population each segment identifies must be large enough to be meaningful, small enough to create some meaningful distinctions between groups, and homogenous enough to be reasonably measured and treated in a consistent fashion.

To help with segmentation development, we've gradually formalized a process of developing and analyzing use cases. At a high level, the complete process looks like Figure 3.2.

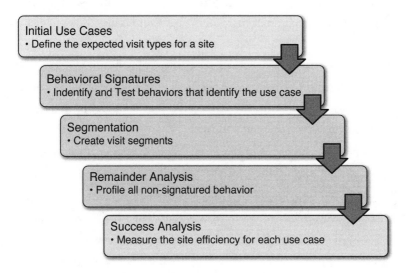

Figure 3.2 The process for creating segmentations

Developing Initial Use Cases

It's possible to adopt a completely data-driven approach to developing use cases. But before we go there, it's important to understand how you might identify use cases without using statistical techniques. That's necessary on plenty of occasions, and it's a helpful way to begin thinking about measuring a digital property. When a digital property first gets built, someone has to decide what it's for, who is likely to use it, and what the website or mobile app has to do for those people. Because it's new, there's no data to work from and no way to build segments in a data-driven way. In this situation, designers tend to think about use cases or journeys when they construct a digital property. If they're good at their job, they work from the business goal to an understanding of potential audiences; then they collect voice of customer (VoC) data to help them understand what those customers care about and what they need from the digital property. When they understand that, they construct a journey map that describes the path (virtual, in our case) a customer might take and what should exist or happen at each step along the way. When we first started trying to analyze digital journeys, we borrowed from the designer's use case terminology and often borrowed the designer's framework. After all, the way the designer built the website is a best-guess approximation for what users are trying to accomplish.

If you've ever immersed yourself in art or literary criticism, you probably remember debates on the importance of the artist's intention. A writer might have intended a story to mean something, but that doesn't necessarily make it so. Similarly, just because a designer built a digital property to support a certain kind of audience and a certain kind of task doesn't mean it's the audience you actually have or the tasks they want to perform. Still, that doesn't mean it's not a pretty good starting point. Designers aren't idiots (mostly), and it's reasonable to assume that they've captured a significant chunk of reality when they designed their use cases and the digital assets to support them.

So if you have a prebuilt set of design use cases when you start analyzing a digital property, it's not a bad idea to use them as your starting point for building behavioral use cases. It's not a big deal if you don't have those preexisting design use cases, though; they're easy to re-create by walking through the site. A formal site walkthrough starts on a key landing page (the open on a mobile app or the home page on a website) and then works through each significant block of content on that page. For each content block, ask yourself who this might be intended for and what use it might fulfill. Next, follow the links and do the same thing. As you categorize each piece of content along a link path, you'll naturally create groupings of related content that form either a single part of a larger purpose or a set of steps on a larger journey. Don't forget to walk through menus, footers and headers, and all that other subterranean content that lurks on most digital properties. Usually, you can analyze these pieces quickly. You can also use quick volume numbers (overlays are nice for this) to eliminate content and paths that have too little volume to be interesting. This might seem contrary to the message around signal-to-noise, but as a practical matter, cleaning up every source of noise isn't realistic. What's more, you'll often find that odd content paths get naturally bucketed (either by data-driven segmentation or because they fall through the hierarchy of a rules-based segmentation) into a grab-bag segment of miscellaneous "all other" behaviors. If your site is one with thousands or hundreds of thousands of pages, you're probably thinking this type of walk-through is either non-exhaustive or totally impractical. That's right. A publishing site, for example, might have hundreds of thousands of "article" pages, each of which is distinct but lives in only a few common templates. For this type of walk-through, you'll probably think no deeper than the template level when evaluating use cases.

In building use cases, you're looking for types of visits in which the consumption pattern (what people will want to view) or the success rate is different. The consumption part of this is pretty obvious. Intent drives consumption, and different intents almost always drive different consumption patterns. The importance of different success rates is less immediately clear.

If two visitors arrive at a website and each claims to be considering buying a product, should the fact that one user is more or less likely to convert drive a use case? There's plenty of room for disagreement in any specific case, but in general, some good reasons support answering this question with a *yes*.

Use cases help us understand success rates, target personalization, and drive subsequent analysis. For each of these, a preexisting likelihood to succeed in some part of the population is important to understand. If you change content within a use case and measure performance both before and after, the expectation is that the content change is driving the difference. But if shifts in the population are skewing the percentages of people who are likely to convert, then deciding whether internal or external factors are driving the outcomes becomes a lot harder.

A site walk-through isn't magic, and it doesn't comprehend every type of potentially interesting use case. It probably doesn't separate out things like populations with differential likelihood to succeed.

On a publishing site, for example, different kinds of use cases are more likely to be defined by the type of focus a user has when entering the site. Are visitors looking for a specific story, checking for big news in the morning, or just browsing the sports page? Those types of use cases need an extra dose of imagination to understand. Because use cases are business specific, it's nearly impossible to create fixed rules for developing them. Table 3.1 contains a little checklist of considerations that might help spur fruitful use case identification and find those more or less qualified populations.

Table 3.1 Use Case Identifiers

User's previous knowledge	In many business use cases, visitors with different levels of knowledge about a product or service often drive different use cases. If a user arrives on an ecommerce site with a particular product in mind, the chances of making a sale are much higher than if that same user arrives with only generalized product interest or introductory product knowledge. This is especially important in categories with high-ticket items and high purchase thresholds, or with more complex products. You generally won't sell a car to people the first time they see it. Similarly, if visitors arrive at a brokerage site not understanding how 529s work, it's more likely that success is educating them on the basics than enrolling them in an account.
User's previous experience	Particularly in areas such as self-service applications, whether a user has ever done the task can make an important use case difference. A common and powerful analysis for most self-service applications and communities is an onboarding (or first-time user) analysis. In essence, this approach makes separate use cases out of first-time visitors versus regulars. It works because previous experience is a powerful predictor of success in most applications.

User's brand knowledge	When brand is an important component of the buying decision, a critical factor is the degree to which users know the brand. User knowledge can significantly shape what they're looking for and their expectations for the experience.
User's journey stage	In any kind of sales cycle, where a user is in the journey is probably the single most important part of determining the use case. Where you are has a huge influence on where you want to go next. Marketing gurus have dreamed up all sorts of different journey models, and there's not much difference between any of them. Most of the generic ones probably need to be tuned to a particular business or space because making them more specific often improves them. Still, the important point is that if you have two users, one ready to buy and the other barely brand aware, you have two different use cases that exhibit two different consumption patterns and two very different levels of success.
Time of day	Time is often more a clue to a type of use case than a true driver of use cases. I've included it, however, because thinking about time helps uncover a set of use cases that might be shaped a little differently. When I log in to Netflix during my exercise time, that time slot and activity shape my desire about what to watch. Similarly, when I pop open a news site first thing in the morning before leaving for work, that available time slot limits how much content I will consume. Although it's probably more accurate to describe the use case as something like Limited-Time Major News Browsing, it's more understandable and more definable as Prework News Check. For plenty of digital properties, time isn't significant, but it's always worth thinking about.
User's day of entry	Most of what I've just said about time of day is true for day of the week as well. Some activities aren't sensitive to the weekend or weekday, for example, but many are. As with time of day, the use case is never going to be just the day of the week or the hour of entry. A use case such as Saturday User isn't illuminating, but when combined with other behaviors, it can be a core part of understanding what a user is about.

Season	Going from time of day, to day of the week, to season made me smile and wonder whether I should add *generation* or *epoch* to the list, but strangely, neither has ever shown up in a real-world segmentation. Season, however, is real. Season is meant to capture the traditional concept, as well as time-specific periods such as spring break that are vitally important in travel and hospitality applications. Knowing that someone is looking for a travel opportunity during spring break is huge if you're trying to understand that user's intent, with all it implies (goals, desires, constraints, and so on) and you want to pick the best offer to show or determine the right sort order for destinations to highlight.
User's focus	Digital tends to be a pull medium. Users pick when and where they want to engage with digital properties, driving most digital properties to provide highly focused experiences. But sometimes and on some sites, a key part of understanding user intent is understanding how focused users are on a specific task or outcome. Someone visiting a healthcare site to check on a lab result is highly focused. The same is true for someone visiting an investment site to unload a stock. The same visitor coming to the same site because he or she clicked through on a fun social media link is much less focused on a particular task. In the first case, the defining fact about the use case is the task itself. But in the second case, the use case can be better described with some type of unfocused browsing categorization. Understanding how broad the user's focus might be can help you set appropriate business goals for a user's session and set appropriate corresponding metrics. The more focused a user is, the more the success metrics need to match the specific activity. The less focused a user is, the more room there is for the business to measure success by engaging the user in other activities or interests.

Creating Behavioral Signatures

All of this just gets you to the point at which you have a set of possible use cases to think about. Those use cases might turn out to be real, but it's also possible that they aren't common or important. You have no way to decide that in the abstract; it's a question of how often that use case is actually occurring in the digital world. To figure that out, the next step is to translate a use case into a segmentation rule.

You have a lot of different ways to do this, and those ways depend on the types of tools and the degree of data access you have available.

In most of the current generation (circa 2016) of tools, segmentation is done in digital analytics tools by stringing together if-then rules about content consumption, entry methods, success events, and similar data points. Even if you have more data-driven statistical methods available, it's important to understand how this process of creating behavioral signatures works. Using the if-then filtering rule is a pretty natural way to go about that.

On one hand, you have an abstract definition of a use case. It might be something like this:

> **Early-Stage Product Research Visit:** A visitor who comes to the website to find out more about a product category, and perhaps to begin to hone in on a particular product or small set of products

That's a compact and business-meaningful use case specification. As always with digital analytics, however, there's no direct counterpart to this in the behavior we can track. The process of creating that mapping typically involves listing all the behaviors that we might expect someone in this use case to show, as well as behaviors that indicate they aren't in this use case.

For our early-stage product research visit, the list might look like this:

Potentially indicative behaviors

- Going from the home page to a product category page
- Landing on a product category page
- Spending large amounts of time on a product category page
- Looking at many product detail pages
- Returning to a smaller subset of product detail pages

Potentially excluding behaviors

- Entering on a product detail page
- Using an internal or external search for a specific product
- Looking at only one product detail page
- Spending very little time on the product category page

Keep in mind that a lot of other behaviors presumably have nothing to do with early-stage shopping (visiting an update account information page, for example). These aren't listed as exclusions, though. The excluding behaviors are typically designed to separate this use case from other use cases that might have the same positive indication behaviors. In this case, we're trying to separate the difference between early-stage and later-stage shoppers. If a visitor uses internal search for a specific product, then that user has already done some early-stage shopping. A visitor might still look at multiple products and go from the home page to a category page, but the search behavior tells us that the visitor is not in the earliest stages of product research.

These types of rules are easy to translate into simple if-then logic of a pseudocode form. A rule for early-stage shoppers might look like this:

```
If Visit Includes (
    (((Entered on Home Page & Next Page was Product Category) OR
    (Entered on Product Category Page)) OR
    (Time Spent on Product Category Page > 2 x User Average for
Product Category Page))
    AND
    (Number of Different Product Detail Pages Viewed > 2)
    AND
    (Number of Product Page Detail Viewed More than Once) > 0 AND
(Number of Product Detail Viewed More than Once < Number of Dif-
ferent Product Detail Pages Viewed)
    )
```

Whew....

I've been profligate in my use of parenthesis and Boolean logic in this example, to make it read as easily as possible, but it's still a mouthful. Here's a version written in something a little less code like that might be easier to scan:

> If a visit:
>
> Started with OR went directly to a Category page OR spent a lot of time on a Category page AND viewed 3 or more Product Detail pages AND showed deeper product interest by viewing some subset of those Product Detail pages more than once...
>
> Then the visit is an Early-Stage Product Research one.

If you're not comfortable with the pseudocode version, it's worth going back and forth between the two versions a few times to make sure you understand how the two map. Even when you understand the mapping, I hope you're at least a bit skeptical. The places I've chosen to group and the choices I've made between *AND* and *OR* are somewhat arbitrary. It would be perfectly reasonable to rewrite the rule this way:

> Started with OR went directly to a Category page AND spent a lot of time on a Category page AND viewed 3 or more Product Detail pages AND showed deeper product interest by viewing some subset of those Product Detail pages more than once...

This way makes sense, too:

> Started with OR went directly to a Category page OR spent a lot of time on a Category page OR viewed 3 or more Product Detail pages **in a single Category** AND showed deeper product interest by viewing some subset of those Product Detail pages more than once...

Each of these three versions produces a different segment. Right now, we have no way of deciding which of these is the closest to reality. I phrased this last sentence as delicately as I could to suggest that there's no "right" answer. Not only are we constrained in our knowledge (so that we can only guess, in most cases, whether a visit is in a use case), but it might not be obvious which use case definition fits best even if we had full knowledge. Suppose we could sit down and talk in depth with each user of the site. Some people will certainly be borderline between early- and later-stage product research. Even the visitors might not be able to easily decide which use case better represents their state of mind.

In building these behavioral signatures, the best approach is to flag places where you're least confident about the logic, grouping, or thresholds of the definition. Those are places to try different versions of the rule to see how they impact the resulting segments.

Before we take that step, however, it's worth thinking about the thresholds built into the definition. Our original working definition contained at least two arbitrary thresholds:

```
(TimeSpent on Product Category Page > 2 x User Average for Prod-
uct Category Page))
AND
(Number of Different Product Detail Pages Viewed) > 2
```

The first threshold is designed to capture the idea that the user spent more time than average on a Category page. We'd expect a late-stage shopper to spend less time on Category pages and more time on Product Detail pages, so the thought is that anyone who spends a lot of time on the Category page is still thinking about different products and, therefore, is in the early stage. But the 2x factor chosen was simply pulled from a hat, which doesn't seem like a very analytical way to approach the problem.

With data-driven segmentations, this isn't an issue. For rule-based segments, though, we should be able to do better than making up a number. Two common techniques work for picking out thresholds in the data that might be useful for this type of definition. The first is to create a distribution of the Average Time Spent per Product Category Page (see Figure 3.3).

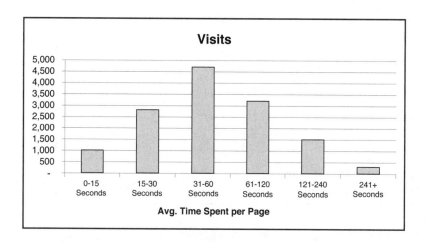

Figure 3.3 Distribution of visits by average time on product category page

In this case, the most common amount of time spent on a Category page is 31–60 seconds, and we have a pretty traditional distribution around that. Anyone who spends more than a minute per page is above average; anyone who spends more than 2 minutes per page is well above average. Given a distribution such as this, we'd probably pick something like 121 seconds as the threshold and change our rule to this:

```
(Time Spent on Product Category Page > 121)
```

This is still an eyeball method, but it's a significant improvement over just making up a threshold. When you translate your pseudocode into an actual segmentation definition, it's much more likely to capture a set of users that feels right.

A more rigorous but still easy-to-use method is to calculate the Average and Standard Deviation of the Time Spent on Category Pages and then put together a distribution of visits based on their number of standard deviations from the mean (see Figure 3.4).

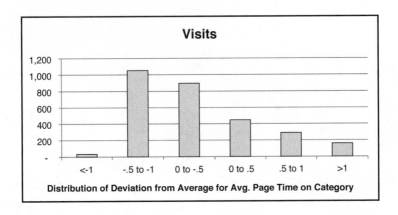

Figure 3.4 Distribution of visits by average time on product category page using standard deviations

It's not unusual to pick a .5 or 1 standard deviation as a cut-off in a variable, and in this case, either might be plausible.

How might you choose between these two values? Having some independent variable to help you decide which of these values produced a more accurate representation would be nice. And yes, you have some ways to get to that variable. For now, though, think about why you might want to make a business decision on where to set this variable.

Essentially, what's at stake in this particular decision is whether a visitor gets assigned to an early- or late-stage shopping use case. For early-stage shoppers, the measure of success is likely easier to achieve—something along the lines of moving them into deeper product consideration or narrowing the set of possible products. For late-stage shoppers, the measure of success is likely conversion.

Depending on where you set the threshold here, you'll fold fewer or more shoppers into early versus late stage. You might then want to think about whether, from a business perspective, it makes sense to be more generous about early- or late-stage shopping segmentation and define the segmentation rule accordingly.

We face a bit of conundrum here. The goal of these segment definitions is to capture reality, not to force business decisions. In the real world, the choice rarely turns out to be quite so pure. It's always worthwhile to try to make good analytic decisions, but when you have legitimate ambiguity, there's nothing wrong with consulting the business consequences of the choice and picking a solution that you think works best for the organization's goals.

Segmentation

Translating the pseudocode definitions developed in the previous step into actual segmentation definitions is the next step. This might seem pretty mechanical, but plenty of gotchas surface here as well.

The first difficulty you're likely to face is a tool dependency. If you have direct access to the digital data stream and can build segmentation rules in an algorithmic language, then you can conceive and document pretty much *any* segment definition. It might not be easy, but it should be possible.

On the other hand, if you're working inside a digital analytics tool, you'll likely have at your disposal a segmentation builder that allows you to construct certain kinds of rules but probably won't allow you to build any rule you can imagine.

Given our original pseudocode, digital analytics tools might struggle with several pieces:

```
If Visit Includes (
    (((Entered on Home Page & Next Page was Product Category) OR
    (Entered on Product Category Page)) OR
    (Time Spent on Product Category Page > 2 x User Average for
Product Category Page))
    AND
    (Number of Different Product Detail Pages Viewed > 2)
    AND
    (Number of Product Page Detail Viewed More than Once) > 0
AND (Number of Product Detail Viewed More than Once < Number of
Different Product Detail Pages Viewed)
    )
```

Yep, we have a lot of potential problems. Depending on the segmentation tool you have access to, you might not be able to properly define a wide range of definition criteria, including these pieces:

- Time-based criteria
- Comparative criteria between two variables
- Statistical criteria
- Criteria based on abstract categories such as Different Pages or Category Page

Fixing this type of problem sometimes involves doing a little more work in the implementation. Different systems allow for different types of rules based on variable types, so if you move data from one place to another, you can sometimes create rules you couldn't before. In addition, many systems place weird limitations on predefined variables such as time; you often have to move them to less restrictive variables to get all the manipulations you need. Likewise, creating additional variables that track abstract concepts such as Category Page can make new and better segment definitions possible. We talk more about the role for this type of variable in the next chapter.

Other times, you just can't get the job done with the tool you have. What are your choices? Get a new tool or change and simplify your rule.

In an ideal world, you have a real advantage when you build your initial behavioral signatures without regard to the types of segmentation your tool can perform. It's an approach that's more likely to get you thinking about what you need in the implementation, and I think it ultimately drives better segmentations. If you're an experienced tool user, however, it's pretty hard not to take your tool's limitations into account when you build those initial segment signatures. It seems a bit fantastical to build definitions you know can't work and then translate them into something that you can implement in the actual tool you have. Thus, there's a strong and probably unavoidable tendency to think about segments in terms of the data and tool you have available.

Just try to be flexible enough to consider whether different approaches to the data and variable capture might help resolve some of those limitations and get you closer to the ideal segment you'd like to have if your toolset and current implementation weren't an issue.

Tool issues will always be with us. Although the current generation of segmentation builders leaves a bit to be desired, most are powerful enough that you can usually find some reasonable proxy for the rules you really want.

So far, everything has focused on building a single segment definition. Obviously, every site will have multiple segments. When you implement a complete visit segmentation, one of the biggest decisions you'll need to make is whether the use cases need to be mutually exclusive. If the answer is no, each segment definition can be completely independent. But if the answer is in favor of mutual exclusivity, each segment definition has to be created in such a way that a visit can be assigned to only a single use case.

Before we discuss the technical details of mutual exclusivity, let's consider the broader implications. It's perfectly possible for a user to do more than one type of action on a digital property. On a brokerage site, I might execute a trade, research a mutual fund, and check my account balance. Those are three distinct site actions. It's possible, even likely, that I arrived at the site fully intending to do all three.

At the same time, the way I navigate the site and the options I choose might suggest that not all of these actions were actually part of my original intent. Suppose, for example, that when I log in, I see an overlay message letting me know that my email address is out-of-date and asking me to update my account. I click on the suggested link and complete the update, and then I go to the trading tool to execute a trade. In this scenario, updating my account was clearly not the use case when I came to the site. We'd be more likely to consider a success event created by site content within a broader use case.

The scenario would be completely different if I logged in, proceeded to my account page, updated my email address, and then, unprompted, went to the trading area.

Site behavior is a complex set of interactions between what users intend and the world that is presented to them, including the available links and the structure of the content viewed. So when a user has more than one type of behavior in a session, it's always worth considering whether those behaviors are really separate use cases or whether the content on the digital property intentionally helped create and drive the additional behavior. When the latter is true, we might consider the additional behaviors as a kind of success metric for the original use case. Cross-sells, upsells, and internal marketing drivers are all examples of this kind of behavior modification.

Still, as long as we admit that sometimes users arrive at a digital property intending to do more than one thing, then having mutually exclusive use cases is, at best, a rough approximation of reality. By letting each segment definition exist independently, you're covered for multiple use cases, although it still is important to properly address issues such as the prompted account update described earlier.

Unfortunately, nonexclusive use cases have at least one significant drawback. Part of building a comprehensive site segmentation is to answer core questions about a digital property, including how it's used and whether it's successful. A comprehensive segmentation is critical to answering those questions well.

It's a truism that executives don't need or want to know the details of every problem. A Chief Marketing Officer (CMO) of a big company probably doesn't need to know which keyword in the PPC program has the best conversion rate. That CMO probably does want to know the answer to this question: Is our website successful? Questions at this level of abstraction don't always make sense—in fact, all our earlier examples were designed to show that you *cannot* answer this question without introducing a segmentation. You have to add "for whom" and "at what" before the question actually makes sense.

Because a digital property has multiple functions and multiple users, it might be successful for some functions and users but a complete failure for others.

This is a long way around to the problem of overlapping segments. When a segmentation is used as the core of a reporting system for site success, overlapping segments create a situation in which use cases outnumber visits. That can be a problem. Report consumers tend to hate it when the line items in a report add up to more than the total.

To avoid this, we have often built our use case segmentations to be mutually exclusive, creating a hierarchy of the segmentation rules in which each segment definition excludes all the visit types defined above it in the hierarchy.

A segmentation hierarchy might look like this:

- Job Seeker

- Customer Support

- Late-Stage Shopper (Met Shopping Definition and Not a Job Seeker)

- Early-Stage Shopper (Met Early-Stage Definition and Not Late-Stage or Job Seeker)

- Brand Browsers (Met Brand Browser Definition and Not Early- or Late-Stage Shopper or Job Seeker)

This can get painful. Where segment definitions are complex (particularly when a tool doesn't allow for encapsulation of the rule), it can mean building all sorts of complex exclusions into the rules at the bottom of the pyramid. If a site has 10 or 12 use cases, the exclusion rules for the lowest-ranking use cases can be absurdly complex.

Ordering the segments also requires careful thought. In the previous example, I put Job Seeker at the top of the pyramid. Why? Well, if someone is looking for a job, that search is probably driving all that person's behavior. Job seekers are notorious for consuming all the content areas on a site so that they can prepare for a job interview, and that can make them look as if they fall into numerous other visit segments. By putting Job Seeker at the top, we ensure that every other segment will exclude anyone classified this way. Not every decision about hierarchy is so clear cut. The hierarchy puts Customer Support next, above all the various shopping life-stage segments. It also organizes the shopping stages so that the most advanced stages trump the less advanced stages. Both are decisions we would commonly make when creating mutually exclusive segments.

To illustrate how complex this can be, however, consider two real-world examples involving customer support and product shopping.

In both cases, we found a high percentage of visits that involved product category and detail page views, along with high customer support page views. In the previous ordering, these visits would all be categorized as Customer Support. In fact, that would have been correct for the first use case. There, it turned out that one of the core product support functions required a model number that was easiest to retrieve by navigating to the product detail page of the website. In practice, that meant quite a few customer support users switched over to the product sales pages during their visit, got that data, and then returned to customer support. By drilling into the order of events, it was clear that the use case was exclusively a customer support one, with no reason to think that any selling was happening here.

The second case played out differently. In that case, we saw a group of visitors who started in the product section and consumed nearly all the content there. Then they hopped over to customer support, searched the product, and browsed the community support there. Nearly always, they hopped back to the product section and had a fairly high conversion rate. Savvy users were checking out the customer support site to check out potential problems before they actually bought something.

We can learn a lot here about the importance of the order of events when creating segmentation rules, but we also need to consider the complexity of segmentations. Users who consume both customer support and product marketing pages might reasonably be seeking both customer support and a product purchase, might be only buying, or might be only looking for support.

I've come to realize that comprehensive mutual exclusivity isn't usually worth the trouble. In addition to all the extra complexity it can bring, mutual exclusivity seems to put artificial boundaries on describing the user journey—particularly in mobile applications, where it's harder to see how traditional web-counting artifacts such as visits really apply. The more "visit" looks like an artificial construct, the less attractive it is to jump through segmentation hoops to tie out to its count.

To address this, we've tried to focus more on a "unit-of-work" concept than a visit. The idea behind the unit-of-work is really a use case. But now, instead of saying that a visit has only one use, we're more likely to say that a visitor has one or more concurrent use cases, that a use case can have one or more touches, and that the most interesting answer to the question, "How successful is our site?," is one in which use case is independent of the traditional concept of a visit.

Of course, to get there, you have to pretty much abandon current digital analytics tools. They are still heavily attuned to the traditional visit concept, and that concept is built deeply into their segmentation and reporting capabilities.

Deciding to abandon comprehensive mutual exclusivity isn't the same as making every segment completely independent. In the earlier examples, it would still be prudent to eliminate Job Seekers from every other segment definition. It would still be necessary to decide among the three alternative versions of what's happening when a user views both customer support and product marketing materials. However, when you abandon mutual exclusivity, you don't have to make *every* single segment exclusive.

Building the actual segmentation rule isn't the whole story. In the examples involving customer support, the overlap between these two behaviors wasn't something we'd considered in either case. It showed up only after the segmentations had been built and we were trying to validate them. That illustrates how important it is to examine the population that results when you implement the segmentation, to see if the behavior contained within is what you expect and to examine carefully cases in which it isn't.

How do you that?

The best way to do quick validation is to set up a standard profiling report that creates a series of index variables comparing the segment to the overall visitor population across a set of key dimensions. Essentially, you're looking for a snapshot of how a segment behaves, compared to the average—where it over-indexes and where it under-indexes.

The report should typically include content consumption metrics across every significant category; overall usage metrics; conversion and success metrics; campaign and source distributions; and, where available, any key customer type, relationship, or demographic variables.

If you build a standard report for this, you can later change just the segment you're filtering on and get a nearly instantaneous and trouble-free profile for any segment. It's worth the trouble. (See Figure 3.5.)

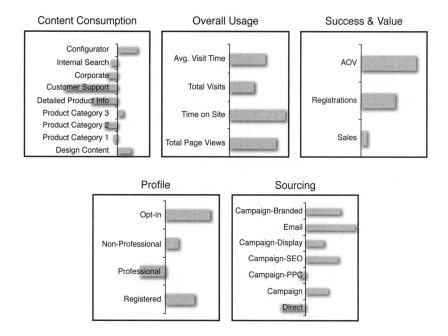

Figure 3.5 Sample segment profile report

With a report like this, you can quickly see where a segment is strong or light in terms of behavior. By looking at different types of content consumption, you can spot unusual patterns such as an increase in customer support pages for a marketing use case.

Remainder Analysis

After you create and validate all the initial segments, you have another step that's easy to miss but is actually one of the most fun and interesting parts of the process. Unless you've been either extraordinarily lucky or (more likely) sloppy in your segment definitions, when you've coded your last segment and you add up all the visits or units-of-work, you'll see a healthy chunk of behavior that doesn't fall into any use case.

One big chunk of that population is often one-and-dones, visitors who land on a single page and then leave. In rare instances, a one-and-done behavior can be classified—for example, the page is accessed via external search and has distinct content (such as an article or a customer support page). In that particular case, even a single page view is likely sufficient to establish a use case. But when a visitor shows up on a general page, especially the home page, and then leaves, it's impossible to determine the real use case.

Several strategies work for dealing with this group. Some analysts prefer to designate them as Unknown or create a use case such as Fly-by and group all the visits with no distinct characteristics into this separate bucket. If a site has a dominant use case, some analysts include this one-and-done population in that use case, under the working assumption that most of this traffic is "failing" in the dominant (anonymous) use case. That's particularly likely if you can show that a majority of the one-and-done population is sourced from marketing campaigns.

Each approach has advantages. From a pure segmentation analysis perspective, eliminating these low-behavior visitors is often cleaner and yields more interesting data. But from a tracking success perspective, grouping those visitors into a dominant use case is more realistic.

If you have a large number of these one-and-dones, then regardless of how you choose to handle them, it's often useful to eliminate them from the profile reporting when you compare segments to the overall distribution. If you don't do that, every segment will over-index on almost every metric, which defeats the purpose of the profile.

Whichever solution you choose for classifying one-and-dones, this isn't the interesting part of the remainder analysis. The interesting step is to look at the group of visitors with significant onsite behavior who have nevertheless resisted classification in any use case.

Analyzing these "remaining" visitors often produces the most interesting findings from a segmentation, and it's not hard to understand why. When you preselect use cases based on either designer templates or a site walkthrough, you're essentially finding the expected uses of the site. In this remainder group are the use cases that nobody thought of and for which the site is often poorly designed. Uncovering these new use cases can be rich analytically.

Pulling out new use cases from the remainder group isn't easy. The best place to start is often the type of profile report shown earlier. Run that for the remainder segment and find areas of behavior that are over-indexed. Next, create a segment from the remainder group based on that over-indexed variable and see what the full set of behaviors looks like.

For example, imagine that the remainder group over-indexes on internal search (not unusual, by the way). Create a subsegment of the remainder group that selects just internal search users. Now profile that group. The profile report didn't include it, but here's a case in which you certainly want to look at the keywords being searched. Few items are more revealing in terms of potential new use cases. For one of my clients, the remainder group had a lot of consumption behavior across all sorts of content areas. When we ran this analysis, we found that most people in the group were searching for a free trial. That wasn't a use case because the client didn't have a free trial, but a significant number of people clearly were expecting or hoping for one.

When you find an interesting grouping, you create a new segmentation rule for it, eliminate it from the remainder group, and then repeat the process. Unlike some activities (such as washing clothes or asking for more budget), this isn't never ending. At some point, you're likely to admit defeat and leave some percentage of visits unclassified or lumped into a miscellaneous bucket. You'll likely never get to 100 percent of visits classified. No hard-and-fast rule governs this, but if you pull two or three new segments out of the remainder bucket, you're doing pretty well. At the same time, you'll generally want to be able to classify 90 percent or more of the visits to the site with any significant behavior.

You've got another option for understanding what these visitors are up to: Ask them. We talk more about the role of online surveys and VoC analytics in Chapter 7, "Voice of Customer, Digital Marketing, and Success Measurement."

For now, it's enough to realize that, at some point, you have to call an end to the remainder analysis.

Defining Success

Regardless of the method you use to define segments, after you create them, you have to define your success criteria. This might seem trivial, and sometimes it is. If you have a segment of potential buyers, success is likely a purchase. But you have a lot of hidden tricks, subtleties, and exceptions to contemplate when you're thinking about success.

A good place to start when defining success is with the user's goals. We often say that the user's goals determine your success. However, your goals aren't necessarily identical to the user's. Nobody comes to a digital store intending to be upsold or cross-sold. Nobody arrives at a website intending to strengthen brand awareness. These are business goals that apply only with respect to specific users in specific situations. You don't upsell someone who doesn't have some intent to buy. You don't strengthen brand awareness without some corresponding interest in content. If someone comes to your website looking for support, your chances of selling that person something are pretty much nil (unless it's a support contract). Your business goal has to be formed with respect to each user's specific intent.

In plenty of cases, of course, your goals are identical to the user's. On most customer support and operational sites, for example, the goal is to help the user self-service as quickly and efficiently as possible. That's what the user wants and is also what the business likely wants. But if you've ever been cross-sold on some new credit card service while you waited to activate your card, you know that, even in support situations, the business goals aren't always completely identical to the user's.

For most sales situations, there is both clear alignment and difference between the goals of the user and the business. The user wants to get the best possible product at the cheapest price. The business certainly wants to sell the right product but has factors such as inventory, margin, and cross-sells to consider. None of this is new or in any way disappointing. One of the great virtues of the digital world is that it largely equalizes the power relationship between buyer and seller. It's understood that each party has its own agenda, and within broadly understood rules (such as price transparency and content accuracy), that's okay.

Starting with your user's goals within a use case helps narrow the range of plausible successes from the business and sharpens your thinking about where your goals and interests might diverge.

As you define success definitions for each use case, keep in mind that use cases are a second tier of a segmentation foundation. The first tier is the traditional "who" dimension that encapsulates demographics, business relationship, and similar types of people-level factors. This top tier can be important in understanding what constitutes success in a given use case.

On a pharma site, for example, one common type of visit is to understand how a drug actually works. If healthcare professionals and patients visit the site, both will likely have this use case, but the definition of success might differ. For a physician, success in the use case involves a deeper assimilation of more technical material than a patient would consider necessary or even useful. The use cases are identical, but the measure of success differs.

This can cut deeply and change not just the specifics of a success measurement, but its very nature. Consider a mutual fund site that sells its products only through brokers. The site likely provides a lot of information about funds, and both brokers and individuals will visit it. One use case will likely center on finding out more about a specific fund, and that use case will be common to both audiences. For brokers, the preferred outcome might be increased sales of that fund or some proxy measure such as downloads of marketing materials. For individuals, the desired outcome might be inquiries about brokers or even just consumption of the fund information.

This type of distinction can cut across almost any visitor dimension. For a shopping site, a segmentation by new versus existing customers might drive differences in success based on cross-sell versus conversion. Overselling prospective new customers is often a bad idea, and the additional friction introduced by cross-selling can cost too much in terms of initial sales. But where you have trusted relationships, you have more opportunities to suggest additional products or services that might be of interest.

An even more common complication arises when it comes to a class of success that can best be described as engagement. If your job is to measure the success of a digital experience, nothing is more maddening than being unable to get an answer to a simple question such as, What's our goal with this experience? You'd think the people who designed the experience and the people who paid for it would have *some* kind of answer to a question like that. But sometimes they don't. More often, the answer is something along the lines of "engagement with the brand," accompanied by either a resigned shrug or a desperate rolling of the eyes. When "engagement with the brand" is the goal of content, it's not uncommon to measure that engagement as a function of content consumption. So success often becomes a matter of whether people consumed the content in some depth.

There's a risk of this becoming tautological, with the measure of success being identical to the definition of the use case. That's a different kind of problem, though. Creating some measure of content consumption that goes beyond mere access is usually possible. You can measure time spent with the content (particularly when the content is streaming), you can measure scrolling (whether the user got to the bottom of the content), you can measure the amount of content consumed (whether there are separate and trackable accesses), and you can measure factors such as repeat consumption (whether the user came back).

Before diving into the weeds, note that it's not impossible to measure actual engagement with the brand. When this kind of goal is either common or expensive, it's definitely worth putting in place the VoC mechanics to do that (see Chapter 6, "Attitudes and Behaviors: Mixing a More Powerful Measurement Cocktail," and Chapter 7). Settling for subjective, made-up proxies for success is one of the great banes of digital measurement; when it matters deeply to the business, it's worth doing the work necessary to avoid this type of strategy. Sometimes, though, it's just not worth it, and you'll likely find yourself creating a proxy for engagement based on content consumption.

When content is being created on a constant basis for a consistent audience, then by far the most pointed and useful test of engagement is repeat consumption. Repeat consumption is a real hurdle. Satisfying it is clear evidence that value was provided and, presumably, recognized. That's a good proxy for engagement.

Repeat consumption isn't always the right measure. If content doesn't change, the amount of content is too small, or the audience targets aren't constant, then it would be unreasonable to expect repeat consumption. No matter how good content is or how brand-engaging it might be, people over the age of 4 won't generally consume the same thing over and over again.

With the spectacular growth in social media, using social shares as a proxy for engagement success has become another fairly common technique. Using social sharing as a proxy measure has some specific advantages and disadvantages. On the plus side, as with repeat consumption, social sharing is a fairly high bar to success. It can apply to content even if it's not refreshed regularly or intended for frequent return. Social sharing is also a strong indicator of brand engagement.

These are all good things. The downsides to social sharing as a proxy measure are that it frequently flags a tiny percentage of the consuming population, it's sensitive to the presentation of sharing options in the UI (which have nothing to do with engagement), and it captures a potentially nonrepresentative sample of content consumers. These are serious limitations. Unless social sharing is a core part of a content experience, it is an unrealistic primary proxy for success.

The next step down is a big one. Time spent with streaming content and multiple-page consumption are each potential proxies for success in content engagement. Each indicates that the user was at least somewhat committed to the consumption experience. Unlike repeat consumption or sharing, however, neither tells you much about the user's perception of the content and its value. Finishing a 30-second video or reading the second page of a story doesn't prove much. Still, these measures have their uses. First, they at least help us understand whether the audience perceived the content to be potentially interesting. Particularly when measuring audiences heavily sourced from marketing campaigns, one key question is whether the audience landed had any interest in the actual content. Used this way, these success proxies are less a measure of content effectiveness than of the campaign's targeting. In most cases, these measures also divide an audience into reasonable buckets, and they often screen off enough of the population to be at least somewhat useful.

The final step down in the great chain of engagement proxies is to measure time on page and scrolling. Time on page has never been a reliable metric, and the complexity of tabbed browsing, mobile performance issues, and constant browsing behavior has made it even less reliable over the years. In addition, many tools collect time on page only when the user clicks additional content. For landing page experiences, this makes the measure almost useless. Measuring engagement using scrolling is plausible—but most tools don't capture scrolling, either. The idea is that recording users scrolling to the bottom of content indicates that they are reading or absorbing it.

Time on page and scrolling are soft measures of engagement success. This often makes them attractive to brand marketers looking to find an easy way to look good in a measured world. These days, however, decision makers are rarely fooled and the political advantages to using slam-dunk proxies for success are diminished. If they are the best you can do, then they are the best you can do. But if the problem is an important one (for example, you are spending a lot of money on branded digital advertising), relying on this type of super-squishy proxy is foolish. These are measurements best used when the problem isn't important enough to warrant a more compelling solution.

Two final gotchas worth mentioning are including the success metric in the definition of the segment and facing the inevitable potential for gaming success metrics.

Analysts often make the inclusion mistake when building a multi-part segment definition or first constructing use cases. Suppose you're building a segment definition for a pharma site use case of Understanding How a Drug Works. A segment definition might look something like this:

Definition:

Viewed 3+ pages in the Drug Information section OR Viewed the Explore video

AND

Viewed the How It Works page

Success:

Viewed the How It Works page

The problem is pretty obvious. Every single person who meets the segment definition must also have succeeded. That's *never* what you want. The success criteria for a use case must be distinct from the definition of the potential segment.

Taking account of the potential for gaming success metrics is trickier. This isn't a pure measurement problem, but in the real world, you must be aware of it. Suppose we rewrote the earlier rule to remove the How It Works page from the original definition:

Definition:

Viewed 3+ pages in the Drug Information section OR Viewed the Explore video

Success:

Viewed the How It Works page

This definition is intended to capture a certain set of behaviors on the website as constructed. But a clever designer might look at this and see an opportunity to create a very successful campaign: Add the Explore video to the How It Works page, make it autoplay, and then create a PPC campaign that lands on that page. Whammo, you have a campaign with a 100 percent success rate. It's just like an election in one of those third-world dictatorships.

We measure the digital world to support better decision making and improved experiences. But just like anything else, measurement can be used for purposes less useful or pure. And just as it's foolish to bemoan that we'd need no government if "men were angels," it is willful naïveté not to account for the possibility of gamesmanship when you construct segment definitions. The whole point of success definitions is to use them to optimize the digital experience and measure performance. So it matters. And if it matters, people will find ways to game the system.

It's impossible to take every eventuality into account, but when building success definitions, consider whether simple changes would make success significantly less interesting or meaningful. Common dodges to factor into your thinking include changing a landing page, adding an autoplay, adding a DHTML page view on an in-page click (to reduce exit rates), repositioning images to drive scrolling, and changing the definition of completion for videos. Because you can't possibly think of everything, and some types of definition are inherently vulnerable to gamesmanship, it's generally necessary to monitor success reporting as well. If you find campaigns that look too successful, match their behavior to the definition to see if the campaign creators have creatively doctored the experience to manufacture the measurement.

Finally, I can't end this section on defining success without looking at the general use of proxies for success and the potential to deepen the nature of the measurements we take in the digital world. To optimize a digital property, you need to understand whom it works for and when it works. That's the whole point of this extended deep dive into two-tiered segmentation. But the definition of *works* is surprisingly challenging. The digital world doesn't exist in a vacuum (thankfully). To understand whether events in the digital world result in success, you have to understand what happened outside, in the physical world. Getting the two worlds to tie together is always hard, not least because we use different measurement systems in each. Solving this type of problem is all about "closing the loop" on measurement so that success can be correctly matched back to the previous behavior. When you can't close the loop, there's a good chance that you can't optimize efficiently or correctly.

Consider a common example of a closed-loop problem. A company takes orders via both its call center and its website. It runs a lot of TV advertising, and the ads show an 800 number and a website address. When you reach the website, you can get more information or fill out an online application. You can also call an 800 number that's listed on every page of the site.

The company runs two new digital campaigns. Campaign A produces 5 percent more online orders than Campaign B.

From this, what can we conclude?

  A. Campaign A is better than Campaign B.

  B. More people probably called from Campaign A than Campaign B.

    C. More people probably called from Campaign B than Campaign A, so the two are the same.

    D. Even though we've measured everything digital, we can't say which is better.

The correct answer is D. Long experience shows that campaigns often differ in their success rates by channel. Some campaigns source a higher percentage of callers to online converters, and some less. So it's possible that Campaign B is equal to or even better than Campaign A. The point is, we don't know. When you can't close open loops such as this one, measurement is paralyzed. People might make decisions based on the data, but there's really no reason to believe they are correct. If those decisions are challenged, everyone is back to gut-feel arguments.

Understanding how connecting online to offline creates challenges and problems isn't hard. There's just no direct tie between browsing a website and walking into a store. And although we have many ways to create those ties (see Chapter 6), none always works. What's surprising is how often closed-loop problems exist even when measurement is entirely within the digital world and we can, in theory, track everything.

As an example, imagine that you're running a Pay-Per-Click (PPC) program to acquire new customers for an online-only baby products store. You test two different PPC creative strategies with identical costs and placements. Campaign A produces 1.5 percent conversion, and Campaign B produces 1 percent conversion. From this, you conclude:

    A. Campaign A is better than Campaign B.

    B. Campaign A converters probably spent the same amount as Campaign B converters.

    C. Campaign B converters probably had a higher Average Order Value (AOV) than Campaign A converters.

D. Even though we've measured digital conversion rates, we're not sure which campaign worked better.

Hint: The answer is always D. Once again, experience suggests that different creative content often sources visitors with distinct conversion rates and average order values—there's no particular reason to expect that those two factors correlate positively. If your goal is to maximize revenue, conversion rate isn't enough.

It's not hard, of course, to just push this to the next level—with digital conversions, we typically measure revenue as well. Now you test two different PPC creative strategies with identical costs and placements. Campaign A produces $1.43 per dollar spent, and Campaign B produces $1.41 per dollar spent. From this, you conclude:

A. Campaign A is better than Campaign B.

B. Campaign B converters probably had the same profit per item as Campaign A converters.

C. Campaign B converters probably had a higher profit per item than Campaign A converters.

D. Even though we've measured digital revenue, we're not sure which campaign worked better.

Here, the issue is that profit might skew differently than revenue, and if campaign sources visitors focused on different types of products, their respective profit margins may be very different per dollar of revenue generated. If only the SATs were this easy.

It doesn't stop here—in fact, things get kind of interesting at the next level. Suppose that you bake profit into the equation and try again.

You test two PPC creative strategies with identical costs and placements. Campaign A produces 7 cents profit per dollar spent, and Campaign B produces 6 cents profit per dollar spent. From this, you conclude:

A. Campaign A is better than Campaign B.

B. Campaign B converters probably have the same propensity to return and spend more as Campaign A converters.

C. Campaign B converters probably have a higher return and purchase propensity than Campaign A converters.

D. Even though we've measured frigging *profit*, we're not sure which campaign worked better.

Why is D the right answer? It may be that Campaign B sources visitors are much more likely to remain as customers. Even though its initial source/visit was slightly less profitable, Campaign B might still be better than Campaign A. What makes this level more interesting is that, unlike the previous cases, there's no simple solution for closing this particular loop. Analysts often use the idea of lifetime value to solve this particular sort of problem. The idea is that we predict the lifetime value (LTV) of a new acquisition and award that to the campaign that drove the acquisition. But LTV is just a guess—and to make a good guess, we need data points that are predictive and known around future LTV. Because we just rolled out our PPC campaign, there's no way to be sure if, two years from now, the campaigns will differ significantly in terms of the LTV of their sourced responders. That doesn't mean it's hopeless. For example, we might be able to predict their LTV based on the products customers actually purchased, the predicted or known age of their babies, their geo-demographics, or anything else we collected during the conversion process.

All these are potentially valid methods for predicting LTV and closing the time loop. But none is better than a guess. What's more, even if we had perfect knowledge of future purchases with 100 percent accuracy, our optimization knowledge still falls short.

Don't believe me? Well, in recent years, companies have recognized that customers who promote their products with favorable reviews, word of mouth, and social commentary are worth a lot more than customers who don't. Suppose Campaign B sources a group of people who buy cheaper, less profitable products but are more likely to recommend them. If you think that's unlikely, ask yourself why the Coventry Motor Inn in San Francisco outpoints the Intercontinental Hotel on a leading travel review site.

The point comes down to this: Every measurement is a proxy. You'll never have perfect knowledge, and you always have to make some decision about where to stop and what makes an acceptable proxy. Think dating. Just because nothing is perfect shouldn't blind anyone to the fact that some choices are much better than others. And just like dating, as you get older and better at making decisions, you can extend and deepen what you take into account when you make your decisions.

We've walked through a five-step process for building a use case segmentation: develop initial use cases, define behavioral signatures, create actual segmentation rules, perform a remainder analysis, and finally, define your success. Each of these steps is complex in its own right, and the full process is undeniably challenging. It's worth it. These use cases make every measurement and analysis of a digital property better: More pointed. More interesting. More relevant. Working carefully through each step helps produce a robust segmentation that can be used across all sorts of digital measurement tasks, and the process itself will often substantially improve the clarity and crispness of your thinking about a digital property.

4

Customer Identity and Taxonomy

The techniques we've talked about so far make it possible to build a fairly interesting mapping from behavior to visit intent. We can now understand what visitors were trying to accomplish when they visited a digital place. Still, these mappings often lack color and rarely help us understand who the visitor is. So although we've partly solved building the *what* piece of a segmentation, we haven't done much to tackle the *who* piece. To get to a deeper level of meaning in the translation of behavior to meaning, we need to find better ways to use each digital action to learn more about the visitor.

Deepening Our Understanding of Behavior

To see how we can deepen this type of visit intent and understand more about the participants in the digital world, I introduce my fictional counterpart in analytics: Conan the Librarian. Growing tired of the endless slaughter of cult priests and plains raiders, Conan wanders into a town one day and takes a job at the library. He's told that, in addition to checking out books, he should make recommendations to patrons based on their usage.

Conan is surprisingly quick for a sword-wielding and somewhat muscle-bound barbarian. He remembers each patron and is eager to provide helpful advice. Like so many barbarians, however, his early education was poor. Conan cannot read.

After a month at the library, Conan is working on a rather lacklus-ter day. With only four patrons, he is eager to make recommendations to each to improve business. Figure 4.1 shows his view of the world.

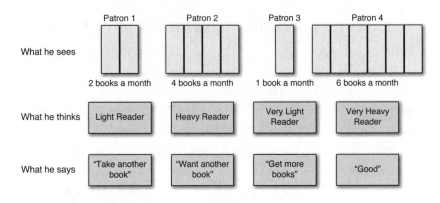

Figure 4.1 The barbarian recommends books

After 30 days, Conan knows all his regular patrons. He hasn't talked to them and doesn't know enough about town life to under-stand much from their dress, but as a clever librarian, he remem-bers exactly how many books each person checked out before and is checking out again. He bases his recommendations on this knowl-edge. Patron 1 has checked out two books this month—not the light-est reader in the bunch, but no deep scholar. Conan strongly suggests another book. Someone with only two in hand can surely use another. Patron 2 is checking out four books. That's not too bad, so Conan is gentler in his recommendation. Perhaps Patron 2 would like just one more? Patron 3 is the lightest reader, and Conan does a little more than merely suggest more books for reading. Patron 4, on the other hand, is the heaviest reader and earns a grudging accolade from our librarian.

No clever man can spend so much time in a library, however, without eventually learning to read. Conan gradually finds himself partaking of the fruits he guards. With this knowledge comes a dif-ferent view of his world. A year later (Conan is a quick study), the weather is particularly fine, the day is exceptionally slow, and the same four patrons happen to return.

Figure 4.2 shows what Conan sees now.

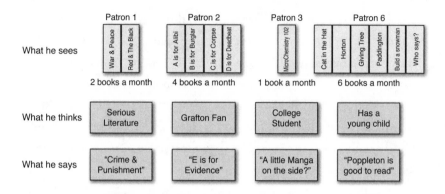

Figure 4.2 Conan the experienced librarian

How different is his view of the world! Light-reading Patron 1 seems to be a consumer of the weightiest literature. Heavy-reading Patron 2 is an enjoyer of lighter fare. Patron 3 isn't getting books for pleasure at all. And the heaviest reader, Patron 4, is checking out books to read to a child.

Originally, Conan's view of his patrons was purely quantitative. He knew only how much they consumed. Now that he understands what people are reading, his recommendations are fantastically more informed. Conan is able to make better recommendations because he can infer from what people read what else they might like. He can even infer something about who they are and what the books are for.

The same is true in our virtual, digital world. Whenever we do digital measuring of any sort, we rely on one basic principle: People's behavior is intentional. What they do tells us about what they want—and maybe a little about who they are. Whenever we measure the digital world, we work implicitly from this principle.

When we measure which pages get viewed more often, we assume that it's because they interest people more. When we measure which pages visitors exit on, we assume it's because they were done or frustrated. When we measure what ads they respond to, we assume it's a measure of interest. Digital measurement assumes intention even at its most basic level.

But a lot of digital measurement doesn't do much better than Conan when he first wanders off the plains and becomes a town librarian. How many pages I consume isn't a great measure of intention. The only thing page consumption might predict is future page consumption—and it isn't a great measure of that. Ditto with how many visits you measure. Exit pages, time on site, time on page—the basic quantitative measures of digital behavior are as uninteresting and uninformative as how many books you check out.

To do better, Conan had to learn to read. Reading gave him the ability to understand more about the choices his patrons were making. He used that information to make better guesses about what else they might enjoy. In making those guesses, Conan was invoking the second most important principle of digital measurement—the assumption that people's preferences are (relatively) stable. We all—everyone and all the time—use this principle constantly and not just in digital measurement.

The single best predictor of what people will do in the future is what they have done in the past. This holds true across a huge range of human behaviors. The best predictor of your grades next semester? Your grades during the previous semesters. The best predictor of what ice cream flavor you'll order next time? The one you've ordered the most in the past. The best predictor of what relationship mistake you'll make this time? The same one you've made in the past.

We all know this isn't always true. People do change. Preferences change. We grow. We shrink, too. People engage in spontaneous acts of kindness and random acts of cruelty. Knowing this doesn't change the basic premise. Past behavior isn't the only predictor of future behavior, but it's almost always the best.

But past behavior tells us something interesting only when we understand quite a bit about the behavior itself. In the digital world, understanding the behavior means understanding the content that is consumed. The first and most important principle that underlies everything we do in digital measurement is the assumption that people's consumption choices are intentional—put simply, that people consume what they want to consume. So if we know what they consumed, we have a true window into who they are and what their intentions were—but knowing what they consumed isn't about knowing the page URL or title. It's knowing what that content is about, who it's intended for, and where it falls in a sales or learning cycle. The more you understand about content, the more you're able to infer about the people who consume it.

This idea of describing content goes by a couple popular nomenclatures. In the broader IT world, descriptions of data are referred to as a metadata. This parlance of metadata is often used to describe the additional things we understand about a piece of content. Classifications of pages into logical groupings are generally referred to as taxonomies. Page taxonomies are a specific type of metadata.

An example of a taxonomy is a set of topics that a page's content maps to. On a sports site, for example, a high-level topic taxonomy might group pages by sport—baseball, football, basketball, and other sports each have a unique classification. Using this taxonomy, a page about the New York Yankees would have a piece of metadata attached to it that tells the analyst the page is about baseball. Not all page metadata is about taxonomies, however. The page might also have metadata that describes how long the content is (number of words or, if video, number of seconds) or the measured reading level of the content.

Classifications and other types of metadata are both important when it comes to describing content for analytic purposes. For segmentation, taxonomic metadata is usually the most interesting and fruitful, but just as some people don't like long books, some people don't like long videos. Form does matter sometimes, and keeping non-taxonomic metadata in mind for segmentation is generally a good idea.

You can categorize content in a surprisingly large number of ways. Most organizations have set up at least some basic content taxonomy variables in their digital analytics solution. Commonly, these taxonomies represent a kind of site mapping with variables that reflect where on the site the page fits. Because sites are organized along broad topic lines, site and topic taxonomies tend to match, at least at a high level.

However, site classifications aren't usually done with enough detail to satisfy the needs for rich analysis. In the sports site example, a site taxonomy typically is organized like this:

Sport
　Pro Football
　　Scores
　　Standings
　　Schedule
　　News
　College Football
　Major League Baseball
　NBA
　College Basketball

Using content consumption to understand visitors based on this type of taxonomy, it's possible to answer questions like these: Which sport is a visitor most interested in? How much time does Visitor X spend on baseball compared to Visitor Y? Does a visitor spend more time tracking scores or reading news or analysis?

These are all great questions, and they definitely sharpen our view of both use cases and visitors. Still, a level of detail is missing. From this type of taxonomy, I can't pick out someone's favorite team. I can't tell whether that team is in or out of the user's geography. I can't tell whether the visitor checks scores real-time or next day. I can't tell which analysts the visitor likes to read or whether the user is interested in fantasy information.

Site taxonomies are intended to facilitate navigation and are based on the assumption that the user's choices merely need to be guided down to a level at which the navigational links can fit onto a single frame. For segmentation purposes, both finer-grained and alternative cuts are often desirable. Matching the site structure affords you an implementation advantage because you can more easily capture the taxonomy, but from a pure measurement perspective, it's better to view topic taxonomies from an independent lens.

It's also really important to recognize that taxonomy selection is not a zero-sum game. Unlike site navigation, you don't have to choose one over another. It's possible—no, desirable and even necessary—to use multiple classification systems when it comes to building segmentations and doing use case analysis.

For example, most sports sites don't organize themselves geographically. But understanding the difference between local and nonlocal topics is a useful segmentation that cuts across every sport (it's useful in a lot of digital contexts). Interestingly, it's also a topic segmentation that differs for each user, so a static Content Management System (CMS) context can't capture it.

Take a look at this cheat sheet of possible classification strategies:

- **Site taxonomy**—Capturing at least three or four levels of site taxonomy is always a good idea, to help describe content. In most cases, this is the navigational grouping of how the content fits within the broader site. It often overlaps with either product or topic taxonomies.

- **Product taxonomy**—The product or product family the page addresses makes up the product taxonomy. For many ecommerce sites, this matches the site taxonomy, but it often has subtle to significant differences. Ideally, the product taxonomy goes all the way down to the level just above SKU, with SKU captured as part of the page metadata for a product detail page.

- **Functional taxonomy**—A functional taxonomy describes pages in terms of their site purpose. Websites (and mobile apps and any digital property) are tools, and each part of the tool is built with a purpose. Functional taxonomies capture that purpose. We dive deeper into functional concepts later in this chapter.

- **Topic taxonomy**—An independent and potentially much more detailed classification than site structure is topic taxonomy. Topic taxonomy commonly crosses a site taxonomy instead of being determined by it. On a sports site, for example, fantasy content might cross a sport-specific grouping. But understanding how much fantasy content a user consumes is interesting regardless of the specific sport. This example also illustrates that, unlike site structure, topic taxonomies need not be fixed and singular. There's no reason you can't or shouldn't have multiple topic taxonomies that overlay any specific page. An article can be about baseball and fantasy—it can even be about baseball *and* football: A story about a stadium, a city, or ratings might well have multiple topic classifications that include both baseball and football and cross-fundamental site structures. Unlike most of the other taxonomies, which assume a fairly rigid structure, topic taxonomies can be formed out of things like SEO keywords, meaning that they grow and change constantly.

- **Audience**—Some content is audience neutral. Some isn't. The audience for *Measuring the Digital World* isn't precisely the same as the audience for *Google Analytics for Dummies*, and it's completely different than the audience for *7 Steps to Becoming a Network Marketing Professional*. Chances are, the content on your digital property is often purpose-built to target specific types of people. A technology site might have content for engineers, content for shipping managers, and content for purchasing agents, all based on the same product, but targeted to completely different people. This type of classification can be uniquely rich in helping profile visitors and determine their role. We worked with one computer hardware site that had a tab on each product page to provide the palette sizes for shipping. It was pretty easy to guess the role of anyone who looked at that content. And it isn't just a matter of role. Sites that have more complex products or services almost always have a range of content designed to help visitors at many different levels of knowledge. Go out and study the content around 529 programs or term life insurance on a financial services site. You'll see content targeting unsophisticated audiences looking to understand what a 529 program is, as well as content aimed at knowledgeable deciders looking to compare choice options between state plans. By coding the audience for a content type and then measuring the mix of consumption in terms of both views and time spent by audience target, it's possible to classify the visitor's knowledge state and even track the evolution of that state over time.

- **Sales stage**—Closely related to audience taxonomies are sales stage classifications. Content can be stage neutral, but where it's focused on a specific part of the sales process, capturing that has a huge impact on differentiating shopper use cases. Depending on your content, you can also shape this as a sales role. Differentiating among pages that focus on price, features, and product comparison can hone in on the key interests and shopping style of a visitor.

These are some of the most common types of taxonomy, but many different possibilities exist, particularly as you consider the specifics of any given site. On a site focused on political commentary, a separate taxonomy might be designed to capture the ideological bent of the content. Does it target conservatives or liberals, Democrats or Republicans? That's hugely important in that context and a powerful tool for appropriate segmentation of visitors.

On a pharma site, a taxonomy might focus on the emotional tone of the content and whether it is meant to be humanistic, scientific, or businesslike.

For a social site, content might be classified in a somewhat different functional way. Is a post about a serious social issue, a humanitarian crisis, a fun holiday, or a product feature? This type of taxonomy is designed to capture the functional tone of a post or a piece of content, and it can be helpful in classifying user responses and building analytics to optimize the editorial mix.

While we're at it, don't forget about the traditional geo-demographic cuts, such as gender and age (or the aforementioned local versus national versus international). Gender, in particular, is a frequent taxonomic classification. Many retailers have huge swaths of products whose target audience is heavily gender biased. That's definitely worth capturing and using as a segmentation variable.

The bottom line is, you can't have too much taxonomy. The richer your classifications, the better your segmentations. It makes the difference between knowing that somebody checked out two books and knowing that those books were *War and Peace* and *The Red and the Black*. It makes the difference between knowing that somebody viewed more than 100 pages last month on the website and spent 13 minutes a day versus knowing that this visitor is a huge Yankees fan with a secondary interest in any New York sports team.

Repeat it: The richer your classifications, the better your segmentations. It should be your mantra.

Taxonomy and metadata are the key to rich analysis of the digital world. Analysts often spend huge amounts of time thinking about which statistical method is the best for any given problem. That's fine. But although these classification exercises might not be sexy, they make all the difference in terms of the richness and quality of the analysis you can perform.

Classifications are the most important type of page metadata in segmentation analysis, but other types of page metadata can be valuable—and are often critical for some other types of measurement.

Here's a quick survey of some common page metadata elements, but keep in mind that these are even more diverse and potentially business specific than classification systems:

- **Page components**—The desire to personalize site experiences and the increasing sophistication of content management systems (CMS) have led to a strong push to create digital pages by assembling various components or modules. This Tinkertoy approach makes it possible to blend different page elements into the view, based on what's most relevant now. Not long ago, every organization was building out these technical capabilities, but nearly all were still delivering a single standard page experience. A lot of talk centered on modularization and personalization, but there wasn't much walk. That's changing. Although the degree of customization is often more of a glossy paint job than a change beneath the hood, a fair amount of page modularization crops up in many digital properties. If the core principle of digital measurement is that what people view is a key part of interpreting their actions, then it follows that knowing what they actually see is essential. Capturing which page components appear to any given visitor becomes necessary.

- **Component description and classification**—Of course, knowing which components are on a page often isn't enough. Just as our librarian could extend segmentation by understanding more about each book being checked out, we gain more opportunities for analysis if we can refine our understanding of what's inside each page component. For example, if a page component is ratings and reviews, then capturing the actual number of reviews and the current rating is extremely useful for many types of measurement analysis. It should be apparent that having this type of page metadata is critical in answering questions on the impact of ratings on purchase performance, but it is also valuable for delving into more segmentation-type questions such as whether a user is ratings sensitive (by analyzing whether the user is likely to view detail, add to cart, or buy products, regardless of rating variance).

- **Product status**—For an ecommerce site (or equivalent), the key elements that describe the current state of a product are absolutely critical for understanding behavior. In one ecommerce analysis, I delved into product conversion rates to study why some products had extremely low conversion rates. It seems like a potentially interesting question, but the answer turned out to be so embarrassingly obvious that it was almost hard to justify spending the money. The products with very low conversion rates were, almost uniformly, out-of-stock items. Visitors couldn't buy the items, so it made sense that conversion rate was low.

  The company commissioned an analysis like this because the implementation wasn't capturing the critical piece of information: the out-of-stock indicator. The company had no visibility into the driver of actual conversion. Most ecommerce sites have fixed this kind of gaping wound in their measurement, but it's still worth pointing out that wherever you have key factors that influence success, you should capture them. For ecommerce properties, knowing when a product is out of stock, which merchandising drives it contains, whether it's being discounted, its price, its product rating, and whether it has images or videos is clearly essential.

- **List size**—Many types of pages contain lists of information: search results, product lists, reviews, and recommended articles, for example. A simple but valuable piece of information is how many items are in the list. For years, analysts have been measuring zero-return searches to help optimize websites. That still makes sense, but it's hardly the only application for this information. In segmenting on sales stage, for example, understanding the number of products returned at each step in a series of faceted searches can be useful. Later-stage searchers often quickly limit the number of products, and the speed at which the user arrives at a small subset is a good indicator of sales stage.

- **Page length**—You can think about page length in two ways. For text-based pages, knowing how many words are on the page is a simple piece of page metadata that can be surprisingly useful both as a segmentation variable and to support analytics for editorial or creative support. As a frequent blogger, I often hear back from folks that my blogs are too long. I'm sure they are. Unlike Mozart, I really can't plead that they are only as many words as I need. The truth is, brevity takes work. It's hard to say something useful with fewer words, and the greater the demand for compression, the harder the task. Understanding content consumption success versus length helps set the bar in the organization for how much work needs to go into a piece. A third dimension is also involved in that question: how long the content piece will be available and how popular we expect it to be. Trimming length on key website content is almost certainly a better investment of time than trimming length on a breakdown of yesterday's midseason hockey game.

The second way to think about page length is in terms of content layout versus device aperture. Knowing what's above and below the fold drives a great deal of UI analysis. As with page components, it's also a key ingredient in understanding what content a user actually experienced.

For sites with dynamic content (publishing sites, social sites, and so on), page metadata about the source of the content should be measured. Details such as the publisher, source, and author are all important, both for the types of analytics they enable (for example, which authors are most successful) and for their potential usefulness in segmentation (for example, it makes a difference whether a visitor consumes Bill Kristol or Bill O'Reilly).

This is fairly obvious when we think about political pundits and visitors who consume their content, but applies in many other areas as well. If you test different versions of a fundraising letter (and you should), one of the key variables is the author. It's always good to have multiple authors pen alternate versions of digital content, especially in transient forms such as email. Almost always, some authors will resonate better with specific segments than others. By tracking author as a key piece of content metadata when testing, segmentation and optimization at this level becomes practical.

This theme has many variations. Tracking content grade level, for example, provides another way to think about both creative/editorial support and segmentation, and video has its own similar but unique set of measurements (play length, resume behavior, segments, resolution, and more).

- **Push date and update date**—Content recency has a substantial impact on performance. In highly dynamic worlds such as news publishing, how recently content was pushed is huge in understanding how much readership to expect. Different types of content even within the same site might age at different rates. On an investment site, general content on investing might age slowly, whereas commentary on the markets might have a lifespan shorter than the fruit fly. Different types of visitors also have different patterns and even specific use cases on content recency. Tracking content recency supports better measurements of true performance at the content level and opens up some potentially interesting (if clearly secondary) options for segmentation.

This barely scratches the surface of page metadata. The topic is so broad and encompasses so many possibilities that enumerating a useful set of principles about the types of page metadata might be interesting. Although the primary focus of this chapter is segmentation and use case analysis, and classifications are most commonly the keys to developing richer segmentations, it should be clear that even basic metadata such as content length or author applies segmentation analysis. In fact, it frequently enables other forms of measurement that are distinctive and powerful in their own right.

Functionalism

Site, product, and topic taxonomies are all extremely common, and each is a core component of understanding what visitors consume. Surprisingly, however, the taxonomic scheme we use most is one that predates the two-tiered segmentation method. Called functionalism, it harkens at least a decade to some of the earliest attempts at developing a methodology for digital analytics.

The idea behind functionalism is startlingly simple (that's an advantage, not a drawback): Measurement should focus on the purpose for which something is intended. To measure a race car, you clock it on a track. You measure a pickup truck by how well it tows and how much it can carry. You measure a minivan by how comfortably and safely it can carry a troop of kids.

The same is true of digital content. A website or mobile application is a complex tool designed to expose some content or functionality to a visitor. You can measure that functionality as a whole, but more importantly, you can break down a complete tool into its components and ask what role each component plays.

Let's stick with our car analogy for a bit. A car is a complex machine made up of a number of subsystems: the power system, the braking system, the carrying system, the steering system, the electronics support system, the entertainment system, the additional safety systems, and so on. If I want to measure whether a race car is good or bad, all I need to do is clock it on the track. That's a simplification, of course, because reliability, safety, and efficiency all matter greatly to a race car. The main point is the same, though. I can understand how well a machine fits its function by understanding its overall performance. If I'm trying to figure out which car to choose in a race, that macro understanding is likely all I need. On the other hand, if I'm trying to improve the performance of the car, that macro understanding isn't enough. I need to know why the car performs well or poorly. To do that, I need to understand the performance of its individual systems.

For a race car, track performance is a function of its power system, braking system, steering system, and carrying system (largely through weight and drag). Each system, in turn, can be broken down into subsystems. For example, the power system is a complex system of intake, regulation, combustion, translation, and exhaust.

In theory, you could use the performance of each component to predict or understand the performance of the system as a whole. That's not usually how it works, though. Typically, the macro performance of a system is measured independently, and then the performance of the subcomponents is measured. If the two largely agree, we assume that our understanding of the system is correct. If they don't, we assume that we either lack information on a particular subsystem or we are misunderstanding one of the component systems.

In other words, if we think race car performance is a function of four systems, and we improve those systems but don't go faster around the track, then either there's an additional system driving some constraint on performance or we've misunderstood one of the four components and haven't actually improved it.

In this way, careful measurement by component provides a back-and-forth process that helps drive improvement and fosters understanding. Functionalism provides a method for doing this in the digital world. It's a way of breaking down a digital property into subcomponents that we can individually measure and optimize. By comparing the success of use cases against improvements in each component of that use case, the same back-and-forth process becomes available.

What are the components of a digital property? It depends, of course, on the digital property. For a fairly traditional business site, the core components might be described like this:

- An engaging system
- A routing and navigation system
- An information system
- A selling system
- A conversion system
- A support system

Some of these elements are universal. Every site has some form of routing and navigation system, although it's not always important or discrete (blogs, for example, lack much real infrastructure for routing). Nearly every business site has some form of selling system, but not all have a conversion system. Other sites might not have a selling system (government sites, for example), but they might still have conversion systems.

The idea of functionalism is to isolate these systems and then measure them according to their function. For example, if we can measure how well a site engages, routes, sells, and converts people, then in theory, we should be able to predict its overall performance. And if we can improve performance in each of these systems, we should see improvement in the overall performance of the system.

Back in the early days of functionalism, mapping a website into pages and treating each page as a component came naturally. First, websites were all there was. Mobile apps didn't exist, and nobody cared about college communities such as Facebook. Second, websites were just pages. Far less modularization occurred, and most pages were both standalone and monolithic.

So the original functional method consisted of two big pieces: a library of page types (functions) and a set of measurements appropriate to those functions. The page types encapsulated a set of common elements that existed on nearly every website. The measurements were then purposefully designed to measure that specific function.

Functional Page Types

Here's a sample of some of the original functional page types:

- **Engagers**—Pages designed to bring eyeballs into your content. The home page on most sites and landing pages for campaigns are often built to engage an audience, not necessarily to sell or route them in a specific fashion. Engager pages can be compared to the display windows of a department store. Those windows aren't designed to sell you something; they're designed to attract eyeballs and present something engaging enough to draw you into the store.

- **Routers**—The key navigational glue of a website. These pages are typically right beneath the home page and are designed to move visitors to the specific content they want. Routers are distinguished because their content is primarily navigational. Internal search, of course, is part of the routing system. On small sites, routers might be an insignificant part of the overall experience. For large, complex sites, however, routing efficiency might be the single most important part of a successful site experience.

- **Informers**—Pages designed to provide information about a product or service. These aren't selling pages. On a financial services site, pages describing term life insurance or a 529 account are informer pages. Measuring a router page by how many people end up purchasing a product after viewing is unreasonable; the same is true of informer pages. These pages often help select visitors in early-stage purchase use cases.

- **Convincers**—Any pages designed to actually sell or convince a visitor fall into this class. They include product detail pages, price pages, feature pages, and other detailed content centered on a product or service. This group of pages is most commonly measured by the traditional measure of success in digital analytics: subsequent conversion. However, because convincers typically imply a somewhat extended sales cycle, their performance is usually measured across repeated visits, not within a single visit.

- **Subsetter**—Pages designed to capture a faceted search. Subsetters help narrow a list of possible products. In addition to faceted search pages, product comparison pages and some aisle pages serve this function. With subsetters, the key to success is their ability to help the visitor hone in on the right content or product set. The actual subsetting success is usually pretty easy to track; the concept of "rightness" is harder.

- **Closers**—Pages with strong calls of a sales action. They typically also include convincer content, but a dominant call to action indicates that their primary function is to drive the conversion process. Because of the immediacy of the function, the success of closer pages can be measured in the same session and sometimes even on a next-click basis.

- **Reassurers**—Pages designed to bolster the visitor's sense of security and comfort. Pages on privacy policies, secure connections, brand strength, warranty, and return policies all fulfill this function. Measuring success on these pages is tricky. Often the group of visitors who access them are self-selected to be less likely to convert or to have special concerns. In many cases, carefully controlled experimentation is the best way to measure the true impact of this page class.

- **Converters**—Operational processes are necessary to move from wanting to buy something to actually purchasing it. These pages provide the functionality necessary to move through a process—for example, carting, entering purchaser information, or confirming an order. Over time, we've found that this class can extend into a more detailed functional view of form types, for example. Form processes are often described as steps and are sometimes even named that way. We might describe a process as having 20 percent abandonment on step 1, 45 percent abandonment on step 2, and 10 percent abandonment on step 3. This type of description makes it seem like there's a problem with step 2, a conclusion that is wholly unwarranted based on the data provided. Classifying steps by function makes it easier to understand what's really happening. For example, the same process might be described as 20 percent abandonment in selecting a plan, 45 percent abandonment in providing name and credit card, and 10 percent abandonment in reviewing the order. Functional classification of form steps—including Provide Identity Information (name, address), Review and Confirm, Select Options, Express Initial Intent, and Provide Payment Method—makes it easier to compare form processes, explain step measurements, and provide measurements specific to form function.

- **Completers**—A kind of handshake to let you know a process is finished. These "thank you" pages mostly serve to let you know something actually happened in the digital world. Completers are a nice example of the way functional thinking not only helps clarify measurement, but improves thinking about digital content in general. On most sites, the real estate on the "thank you" page is largely unutilized. If someone downloads a white paper on a B2B site, that user often gets a "Download Completed" message. The same is true when you register on many websites or make a purchase.

Yet these are all major milestones in a digital experience. Surely, just saying "You're done" isn't the only (or best) thing that can be said. Because digital provides seemingly endless space, we tend to devalue its importance. Having a shop on Times Square in New York is incredibly expensive because the space is so limited and valuable: You don't put a tire shop there. But we can always add new web pages.

True, we have limitless theoretical digital space to work with, but the presentation space you have is much more restricted. Visitors to your digital property see a single frame that must contain the whole of their navigational options and whatever items you want to put in front of them. That might be what fits on an iPhone screen or whatever slides into a decent-size monitor. Either way, it's far less than can fit into a typical store or even on a typical shelf.

Part of digital optimization and measurement involves constantly asking two questions: How valuable is this space? What can I do to take best advantage of it? For completer pages, the space is uniquely valuable because the audience is self-selected as highly qualified and have, furthermore, provided you with some interesting fact about their interests. Don't ignore that! For completer pages, the measurement we recommend is the number of additional conversations you can create by directed navigation to content suggested on the page.

This isn't a comprehensive list of page types; these types are merely typical of a business or ecommerce site and are paradigmatic of functionalism. As a page-based methodology, it works best on this type of site, but functionalism isn't limited to traditional business sites.

Public service sites have core components that often map well to functional concepts, as do many branded sites. Even customer support and media properties can be given a functional spin. Consider some potential functional types on a publishing site:

- **Dashboards**—Pages that update in real time to track one or more events. Election night trackers and NFL Sunday scoreboards are examples of dashboards.

- **Articles**—The traditional article template when a visitor arrives via traditional site navigation.

- **Arrival article**—An article accessed externally from search that serves as both a site landing page and an article template.

- **Card file**—A page that aggregates all the information on a single topic into a single place and provides structure to the content.

- **Thread**—A page built around a conversational thread, usually a set of comments or back-and-forth dialogue.

Why Functional Measurement Matters

A big part of the goal in building functionalism was driving measurement down to a level where meaningful optimization could take place. Knowing that a car goes 120 mph doesn't tell you what to do to make it go faster. To improve page performance, it's critical that measurement actually work at the page level. For nearly any complex system, the application of macro-measurements to individual systems is challenging. Certainly, in the digital world, it's often difficult to see how changes to a page that lives far upstream in a sales process can impact the final measures of success. Measurement systems just aren't precise enough to see how changing a link on a router page drives the lifetime value of a customer.

So with functionalism, the idea was to measure as close to purpose as possible. If a page was designed to route visitors to the pages they wanted to consume, why not measure its actual performance in that function? In practice, this meant replacing the idea of measuring every page against some end-state success, with the idea of measuring each part of the website differently and according to specific measurements related to subtasks of the website.

For a router page, a functional measurement is the percent of times a visitor who arrives at that page actually uses one of the suggested navigational links in the main body of the page. This isn't the same as a visitor taking any path from the page. If a user clicks the Back button to return to the home page, uses internal search, scrolls to the bottom of the page, and clicks something in the footer or pulls down a main menu link, that user hasn't routed according to the page. Dividing how often a suggested route is taken with how often the page is viewed gives a routing percentage that serves as a measurement for page success.

It's easy to understand why this type of measurement is useful. Given our first principle of web measurement, that what people consume is indicative of what they want, then the more often people click through on a router page link, the more often we've managed to provide the navigation path they need.

It's also easy to see how this type of measurement can help establish a balance. If you have two links on a router page, each can be fully described and clearly delineated. But a visitor has only two choices. Adding choices could make it more likely that you'll include links the visitor wants. But each new link reduces the viewability and space allocated to each of the items presented, making it less likely that the user will find the right link. Somewhere we need the right balance between number of choices and transparency of choice; functional measurement might be able to identify that optimal balance point.

Moving the measurement closer to the function of the page also improves the sensitivity of the measurement. Every real analyst knows that, in the sea of complexity life presents, most measurements don't reveal anything significant. You might make countless small changes to a website, none of which can be measured in isolation as significant for overall success but which, if directionally correct, can add up to a significant change.

The key, of course, is how you can know whether the changes are directionally correct. If you make 100 changes, and 50 of them help and 50 hurt, you might well end up exactly where you started, from a macro-success perspective. If you can figure out which 50 changes worked, however, and implement just those, then you generate real improvement. Functionalism is designed to help measure directional success.

We've spent a lot of time elaborating on page types and specific measurements of the functional methodology, but the most important point isn't what the right measure of a router page is. The key is understanding that if you can make measurement track to function, you have a chance to analyze subsystems in a meaningful way that will work inside macro-performance measurement.

The functional methodology was explicitly designed to be extensible. Nothing is magical about the page types. Having a predefined library of types makes it easy to communicate to an entire community how and why you're going to measure a specific page in a certain way. But a lone analyst working on optimizing a specific use case can just as easily and effectively break down a process into a set of constituent pieces, attach names to each of those pieces, and develop custom measurements for evaluating each piece according to its specific function. Without any predefined page types, measurements, or communication, this is still a functional approach. This method has proven interesting and successful across many years, many different types of properties, and many different analysts.

Implementing and Expanding a Functional Approach

If you're taking a functional approach to measuring the content inside a use case, be sure to keep some general principles in mind. First, pages or components need not be limited to a single function. A home page is often an engager and a router. A router page might have convincer content on it. A page might even change function relative to how it's accessed and/or the variation of the page being served.

Likewise, each function might have more than one associated measurement—or even have the same measurement, but taken in two separate situations. For router pages, the core functional measurement is typically the routing percentage. However, router pages function somewhat differently when they're accessed after drilling down into one of the routes. It's often interesting to measure routing percentage when a router is first accessed versus routing percentage when the page is accessed again after an initial successful routing. Measuring how often the visitor returns down a previously taken route is also interesting.

The general principles behind function description and measurement are fairly simple. Function should be described in terms of the role played in a broader use case process. The measurement should be relevant to the function, differentiable (just as in our discussion of success metrics for a use case, the functional measurement shouldn't be met 100 percent of the time), and, ideally, easy to abstract.

In the original functional definition, the functional measurements had to be easily culled from a digital analytics tool. Back in the early 2000s, people were lucky if they had even that much. These days, with rich direct access to the data much more common, worrying about the complexity of data abstraction is less important. Still, there's not much point to coming up with a measurement you can't capture. If you're trying to perform a functional analysis and you have a digital analytics tool to do it with, it just makes sense to pick the best measurement you actually have available.

The original functional concepts were very much a page-based system. For some sites, that approach still works pretty well, but it's become less appropriate over time. That's part of why we've increasingly relied on segmentation and use case–based approaches. It's not the only reason, of course. We've found that functional approaches work best inside a two-tiered segmentation framework. Otherwise, you're looking at a page and asking if it works well, but you're missing the context of who it works for and when it works well. Even inside a use case foundation, however, the page focus of functionalism feels a little dated.

That's why it's preferable for many sites to take a less page-oriented and more systems-oriented approach to understanding subsystems of digital properties. Instead of thinking about a routing page, think about a routing system that has some full pages but also other components (such as the search box or recommendation modules) spread throughout the site. If a page has routing components on it, you can measure the router performance of the page and the individual components even while tracking separate functional measurements of other aspects of the page.

Taking functional concepts to a system level can change the way the measurement actually works. Instead of measuring routing performance just on a page level, you can measure it within an entire use case. For an early-stage use case, you could measure routing performance by the number of clicks, time taken, and percentage of visitors who get to subsetting or convincing content. You could then further operationalize this overall routing system performance at the page and component level for each piece of the digital property that's commonly touched within the use case.

This approach provides three levels of measurement: the overall success for the use case, the functional measurement for the use case as a whole, and the functional measurement for an individual page or component within the use case.

For the most part, functionalism is a methodology for isolating performance issues inside a use case. However, functionalism as a segmentation taxonomy is surprisingly useful as well.

Functionalism As a Segmentation Cue

Some aspects of use cases and visitors are powerfully illuminated by functional categorization and might not be as obvious as the uses for a topic- or product-based taxonomy. A user who looks at a lot of router pages relative to other categories probably isn't in a traditional shopping or informational use case. Similarly, the more time a user spends on router pages relative to convincer or informer pages, the earlier that user likely falls in the sales process. A visitor who spends little time on a router page before navigating is likely further along in the sales stage. A visitor who spends more time on informer pages than convincer pages is earlier in the sales cycle, and the ratio between these two might well predict the journey stage.

This is just a sampling of the different ways functional concepts can categorize visits into deeper categories. If the core concept behind functionalism is that we must tailor measurement to purpose, the second most important idea is that understanding the way visitors in the digital world use a tool tells us a lot about who they are.

At one time, functionalism was the primary methodology for measuring the digital world. Now it's a much smaller piece of the framework—in some ways, it is nothing more than one of many possible metadata taxonomies for classifying content. That being said, it's still interesting. It's surprisingly powerful and, for many people, unexpected but also obvious. Its combination of power, interest, and accessibility makes it a good way to create a disciplined conversation about content and what it's supposed to accomplish.

Whichever taxonomies you end up choosing to work with, you'll likely find it challenging to get these classifications into your data, where you can analyze them. Metadata itself is data; it doesn't appear from nowhere, and its creation can be a real problem for analysts.

Building Taxonomies

The analyst's job is to design and use taxonomies. Sometimes a well-designed organization takes care of all the minutia of implementing and maintaining a taxonomy so that the analyst doesn't have to worry about how a taxonomy gets created. Sometimes your children clean their rooms, do all their chores, and send unsolicited thank-yous to their grandmothers. Sometimes.

Chances are, that's not always going to be the case, so it's worth a quick look at the ways to create taxonomies.

In that ideal world, taxonomies exist because content creators attach the classifications to the content in the content management system (CMS) when they're first built. As with any data quality issue, the further upstream you can push the creation of metadata, the better off you're likely to be. If the taxonomy is created as part of the content, then it exists in the CMS and can be pushed through to the page as metadata in the Document Object Model (DOM) that describes that page to the web. If it's in the DOM, any digital analytics system can pick it up trivially and store it in a variable, making it available for analysis.

Unfortunately, when a classification isn't created in the CMS, getting it there is usually a big deal. You have to add it to the CMS, train content creators in how to specify it, create it for all existing content, and then modify the digital analytics tagging to snag it off the page. Your chances of getting this done so that you can try an analysis are slim.

Sometimes metadata can be collected from a third system outside the web. For example, products are often described somewhere in the enterprise warehouse at the SKU level. If you can pull a table that contains the SKU and various product attributes, you can match that file to digital analytics data.

Most digital analytics tools have built-in functionality for this type of metadata matching and, of course, if you have direct access to the raw data in a relational DBMS or HDFS system, you can easily append it.

In some cases, metadata comes from a third-party database. If your pages happen to describe some public entity (movies, TV shows, songs, houses, buildings, places, people, and so on), you can use public or purchased databases that include rich descriptive metadata. The integration process is identical, regardless of whether your metadata source is internal or external.

Sadly, the classifications you want (such as functional classification) typically won't exist in any public or private database. The alternatives aren't always great. You have two options for attaching metadata to content: creating it as part of the analysis system or creating your own lookup table that can be appended to the digital analytics solution just as if the file existed externally.

In the first case, your analysis might simply contain programmatic logic that classifies each page. In the second, you'll need to first extract a list of pages and then either hand-code or programmatically classify each page in the file. Then you'll append that file back to the digital analytics data.

If you're creating a functional analysis (as an example), it's often practical to simply hand-code or select a small number of pages within a single system. It isn't necessary or even particularly beneficial to code every page on a site, and nothing is wrong with creating a tiny subset of classified pages based on the system under study and the actual view volumes of the pages. When many pages must be classified, it's often possible to design simple matching rules (using Regex-like expressions) that enable the coding of many pages with a single rule. On a media site, for example, it's not unusual for *every* article page to have a standard URL template, with parts of the URL being very consistent. Creating a simple rule to search for the key parts of that template facilitates coding tens of thousands of pages in one fell swoop.

Sometimes the job of creating a taxonomy is truly analytic. Suppose, for example, that you want to create a different type of product classification taxonomy on an ecommerce site. Instead of simply classifying by price, your goal is to classify whether a brand is relatively expensive compared to its natural product competitors. You could do this by hand, but it would involve a lot of guesswork, based on the way a faceted search (for example) might play out. Instead, you might choose to capture all the product sets returned in a week's worth of faceted searches and then analyze, for every product, whether it tends to be priced high or low relative to the other products returned on, say, the first page of search results.

This is a powerful type of classification and one that we've used when analyzing product search results for manufacturers. It's quite predictive of both product sales success and internal search ranking on ecommerce engines. Obviously, however, it's not a taxonomy that comes ready made. Getting at the data and creating the taxonomy takes a significant amount of data processing work and basic analysis.

An even more sophisticated example involves using text analytics tools to categorize the content on a web page across dimensions such as topic, tone, detail, audience, or level. Extracting an interesting taxonomy from a scan of the contents of a digital property makes it possible to build rich and complex taxonomies on the fly, without any operational impacts. The penalty you pay comes in the relatively steep price in work and skill that comes with any sophisticated text classification effort.

As they mature, most organizations eventually realize that creating taxonomies is a key part of what an analyst must and should be doing. That function comes with a unique tool set that includes page databases, external data, Regex tools, spidering and scanning tools, and sophisticated text analytics systems. It also becomes apparent that not every taxonomy an analyst thinks will be useful turns out to be genuinely interesting. Typically, therefore, analysts first create a taxonomy in a rough-and-ready way and then test it within some specific analytic applications. That test can be almost anything: segmentation, personalization, experience optimization, or offer matching. If a taxonomy proves itself in an analytics test, it can be gradually productionized. Eventually, if it becomes a key part of the way the enterprise thinks about content, it's likely to end up with a place of honor in the CMS, where it is coded for every piece of content created.

In this way, data about data becomes a system unto itself and a huge differentiator in the value and success of analytics in the organization.

Analysts like to think about analytics. Advanced methods and interesting statistical techniques, cool visualizations, and startling conclusions are the dishes we best love to describe and serve. Metadata is boring hard work—not the least bit glamorous. Thinking up interesting taxonomies isn't that much fun, and building them is never anything but a slog. But metadata and classifications make digital analysis possible. They aren't the gravy or the seasoning. They are fundamental to adding meaning to digital structures. No part of measuring the digital world is more important or more useful than the imaginative and interesting ways we find to describe the building blocks of the digital world. When you understand how digital measurement works, the reason for this centrality should be obvious. If by understanding what content visitors consume we can understand who they are, then the better we describe that content, the better we understand our visitors.

5

Website Structure

In the last chapter, we showed how deepening our understanding of what visitors did in the digital world can help us understand who they are. That seems right and is almost always true. But it's not as consistently true as we might like to think. The problem is that digital properties—websites and mobile apps—have a structure. Visitors don't hop from place to place at their will. On any given page of a website, a set of links defines where else in the digital property users can go. What's more, some of those links are *huge* and prominent, whereas others are tiny and buried in the bottom of a long page. This navigational structure makes a profound difference to our measurement strategies because it creates powerful correlations between specific pieces of content and navigation paths. So the assumption that what visitors viewed is what they were interested in needs to be tempered with the realization that the tool we give visitors to navigate the digital space (the website or app) pushes them in specific directions.

Postulate 2: Postulate 1 Is Often Wrong

In this chapter, we consider the profound impact of structure on digital measurement and show how it makes virtually all straightforward statistical analysis of web content consumption useless. Finally, we tackle some methods for handling website and app structure when we do analysis.

If the first principle of digital analytics is that we understand who visitors are and what they intended by studying the content they consumed, the second principle really ought to be this: Beware of the first principle.

To understand why interpreting people's behavior can be problematic, let's revisit the library analogy. When choosing books from a library, it's understood that a patron chooses from the selection available. Given that millions of books are theoretically available, even a large library represents only a small subset of the available choices. Sometimes this is a serious limitation. A patron looking for a book on Hadoop programming might be disappointed with the local library. The same is true if someone is searching for a cycling tour guide to Croatia. On the other hand, if someone is looking for a mystery, a novel, or a children's book, then most times the library selection suffices.

The implication of this is clear: The more specific the patron's intent, the more likely the person's behavior will be either inconclusive (the person won't check out any books) or misleading—the visitor will get something, but not quite what he or she wanted.

For a library, selection is by far the biggest limitation on using behavior to understand intent. However, a second factor can subtly influence behavior. As with any physical building, a library is laid out with a specific structure. Literature is over there. Children's books are in that room back there. Mysteries are off to the right. History books are right there. Science books are in the back. Whatever the layout, it's sure to have at least a small impact on selection. If patrons show up genuinely uncertain about what they want, the placement of the stacks could significantly influence their choice. In most libraries, for example, new releases occupy a prominent entry position.

Unlike a grocery store, most libraries aren't designed to nudge you from your preferred path. They aren't trying to "sell" new releases— they just know that's the most popular single set of books with their patrons, so placing them closest to the entry in a highly visible location is a convenience. But it's a convenience that will certainly shift at least some patrons' behavior. After all, as you walk in the door, you're most likely to check out the shelves nearest to you, and that's particularly true if you aren't strongly disposed toward a particular section.

This type of behavioral shifting is common with all physical structures. Remember, in grocery store design, the layout of the store is expressly designed to force shoppers to traverse large swaths of the store and to optimize certain kinds of impulse purchases.

The digital world is limitless, of course, allowing for endless expansion and essentially unbounded shelf space (imagine Amazon as a store—pushing your cart through the aisles would take a long time). Nevertheless, the digital world suffers from both selection limitation and behavioral shifting. In fact, it suffers (or benefits) from the latter to a much greater degree than most physical structures.

Selection limitation occurs in the digital world because content is limited and can be quite expensive to create or license. You can't always find what you are looking for or need, whether it's the movie you want to stream, the information you need for your travels, or the information about a product or service.

For most digital properties, behavioral shifting is far more important than selection limitation. Digital properties, whether they are websites, mobile applications, or communities, all have a strong structure. That structure is dictated by the constraints and opportunities of HTML digital design and screen size.

On a typical home page, a company might present 50 different links. These links are the pathways available to the users. They can't walk anywhere else—links are like the aisles in a grocery store. But unlike a grocery store or library, where the path choices are presented in a relatively equal manner, most digital properties heavily bias the design toward either popular or profitable pathways. It's not unusual for a single path to take up 40 to 50 percent of the immediately visible screen real estate on a home page, and for 50 percent of the links to take up less than 5 percent of the viewable area.

This structure has a massive impact on the way visitors navigate a digital property. First, it means that it's often impossible for a visitor to get directly from Point A (say, a piece of content) to Point B (a success page). Instead, the user might have to navigate an array of points. What's more, the distance between places can vary widely: It might be an easy single hop between some points but a much more circuitous route between two other points. Finally, the ease of getting to any given point can vary enormously, depending on how someone entered the site. A page that is easily accessed and visible on the home page might be entirely hidden if a visitor enters on a product detail or article template page.

People don't think of the digital world as bounded and topographical, but it is. Navigating a city by car is a pretty natural analogy for a user navigating a digital property. Users aren't blessed with a full-on GPS. They can see large roads and small roads, and they have access to certain special routes (via menus) that function like freeways, moving them rapidly to different points in the city. But without a GPS or even a comprehensive map, visitors have to feel their way through the navigation, trying to choose roads that appear to lead in the direction they want to go. Naturally, the larger and more visible roads are especially likely to be chosen if they show any promise at all.

All of this might seem obvious. It *is* obvious. But if the impact of digital structure on behavior seems almost too obvious to mention, it vastly complicates every kind of measurement and analysis.

It's not unusual for analysts—and even (or particularly) data scientists—to believe that they can measure the success of a web page by measuring its correlation when viewed to a positive outcome. On its face, this doesn't seem unreasonable. It's the way we measure most things.

Unfortunately, it doesn't work because digital properties are highly structured.

I happen to live in the San Francisco Bay area, so I often use the Golden Gate Bridge as an example of how topology trumps correlation. For many tourists, walking the Golden Gate Bridge is a must-do part of a visit. So we can think of getting to the Golden Gate Bridge as a success outcome. Figure 5.1 shows a street map of San Francisco with the Northwestern tip expanded (that's where the bridge is).

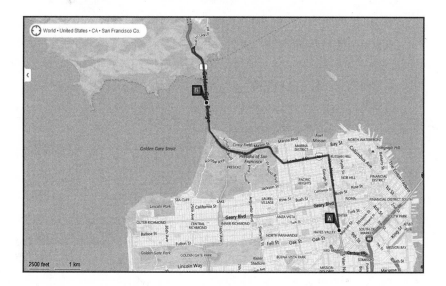

Figure 5.1 Getting to the Golden Gate Bridge

Notice that only two roads lead from San Francisco (in the bottom half of the map) to the bridge. So if you're trying to cross the bridge off your bucket list, you're going to take one of those two roads. What's more, tourists aren't distributed randomly across the city (although it can sometimes feel that way in summer). The overwhelming majority of tourists stay on the east side of the city near the downtown, Union Square, or Fisherman's Wharf areas. If you look at the map, it means virtually all tourists will end up on the same road: the one that leads from the east side of the city to the bridge.

Suppose we correlate using each road in San Francisco with getting to the bridge. That's equivalent to measuring the correlation of viewing a web page with a successful outcome. Naturally, the road from the east part of San Francisco to the bridge is going to be massively correlated with actually reaching the bridge. The road from the south part of the city will be heavily correlated. The major roads that lead into the eastern approach will also be heavily correlated. Indeed, the correlations will spread out like branches on a tree, with gradually diminishing strength the farther they are from the main access roads to the bridge.

In effect, by measuring the correlation of roads to bridge access, we are re-creating a map of the city based on the road structure and where tourists tend to stay.

Exactly the same thing happens if you measure the correlation of pages on a digital property to success outcomes. You don't get a measure of content effectiveness—you get a map of the digital space based on the inherent structure and common entry points. Pages closest and most broadly connected to the success outcomes will have high correlations. Pages that are closely connected to those pages will have reduced but still high correlations. And so on.

Although creating a map of a digital property is interesting and can even be useful, it isn't what most analysts have in mind when they measure the correlation of page viewing with success. The typical goal is to understand whether that content caused success. But in most cases, the correlation no more measures causality than the roads leading to the Golden Gate Bridge "caused" people to go there.

Because structural correlations are so strong, they generally swamp the difference in correlation to success driven by actual content effectiveness.

Structure trumps causality.

Website structure might be obvious, but it's surprisingly easy to forget when looking at the measurements inside a digital analytics or statistical analysis tool. Nowhere is the concept of structure captured in the reports delivered in any out-of-the-box solution. It can be all too easy to forget that apparently strong relationships in the data between behaviors and outcomes are nearly always structural, not causal.

No New Problems—Just Old Mistakes

Earlier, I explained the idea behind two-tiered segmentation in terms of signal-to-noise. The idea is that removing the extraneous noise of behaviors unrelated to the content or purpose in question makes key measurements such as conversion rate much crisper. Similarly, you can think of the measurement foundation I laid out in the first four chapters as a way to solve another vexing and common mistake in statistical analysis: the problem of self-selection.

Self-selection, a huge complication to an "easy" interpretation of the impact of web behavior on outcomes, is worth pondering for a moment. Consider an example.

One of our clients, an investment brokerage, had a small link near the top of its website that read Open a New Account. Unsurprisingly, people who clicked on that link were quite likely to open a new account. That link and the page it targeted were both highly related to a key success outcome. What makes this case different from the structural cases described earlier is that the link wasn't especially close to final conversion, but it still had a high correlation to success. Correlation, of course, does not equal causality. Neither the link nor the page it targeted was causing people to convert. Instead, it was merely letting people convert. This type of self-selection is everywhere in the digital world, and it trumps even structure. It drives nearly every aspect of behavior and makes the basic search for correlation between content and outcome fruitless.

Fortunately, that's not such a big deal to us. Think about it, and you'll see that the logic behind the two-tiered segmentation I laid out in the previous chapters is actually dependent on self-selection. The fact that someone clicked an Open a New Account link on the home page is evidence that this person is in a Ready to Buy use case. A more subtle fact is that part of what makes that segmentation framework a great foundation for digital measurement is that it uses, not abuses, the idea of self-selection. By creating use cases that specifically capture the difference between visitors ready to convert and visitors still researching or learning, the two-tiered segmentation controls for self-selection by using it to define independent groups.

As with signal-to-noise, one way to think about the creation of use cases is to always attempt to isolate different levels of self-selection into independent use cases.

Controlling for self-selection is a fundamental part of our measurement foundation, but controlling for structural impacts is less clearly baked in.

Selection Limitation

The impact of selection limitation is hard to gauge on most digital properties. It's a kind of "we don't know what we don't know" problem. Missing content might well be driving strange use cases or even large-scale abandonment, driving up the rate of one-and-done unclassified behavior. There's just no easy way to recognize this from consumption behavior.

Three main techniques help you get at selection limitation problems: internal search, deep navigation, and voice of customer (VoC).

Internal search has been a staple of digital analytics since the early days of the web. It's not hard to understand why. A search term is inherently revealing about what the user is looking for (at least, when it's not just your brand name). In particular, internal search is revealing because it is *not* constrained by selection limitation. Users are free to enter whatever they want in that little search box. What's more, the ubiquity of search behavior in the broader digital universe means that it's a pretty standard fallback behavior when users can't find what they're looking for.

Five common types of internal search analysis exist. The first is simply to analyze the search terms entered by frequency and look for commonly entered terms that are not well represented in content. A small variation of this is to look for search terms that return a zero result. For selection limitation, zero-result analysis generally isn't a viable approach. Problems with product lookup and similar technical searches often are revealed by searches that return no results. But with today's search engines, it's rare that *any* content-based search won't return some results, however useless and irrelevant they might be.

A second type of internal search analysis uses textual classification to group related searches together and even help form them into use case cues. For sites with significant internal or external search behavior, this kind of classification is essential to integrating search into the measurement foundation. This classification work has the additional benefit of highlighting groups of searches that fall outside current use cases and summarizing their volume.

A third wrinkle in internal search analysis looks at the behavior of the visitor on the search results page. Did the visitor click any result, and if so, what position was it in? Were multiple pages of results scanned or was a search reissued? This type of analysis is typically a way to optimize internal search results themselves. Commonly searched terms that often give results that the user ignores are strong candidates for re-engineering. But assuming that the search isn't merely broken, these same areas are often areas where visitors are experiencing selection limitation. Users just have no good content to find.

A fourth type of internal search analysis takes the after-search behavior a step further and looks at whether the visitors' search results–based content consumption appears to be successful. If visitors commonly click through on a search result but then exit the property or reissue a different search, it's a good bet that either the search tool is broken for that keyword or the content doesn't meet the need. When it's the second alternative, that's a case of selection limitation.

Finally, looking at where on a digital property a search originates can be useful for understanding possible cases of selection limitation. Analyzing search keywords relative to the page on which the search was initiated can make it clear that visitors were looking for something on that page they couldn't find. This, too, can be a good pointer to potential selection limitation issues.

If internal search is an old standby for most digital analysts, looking at deep navigation is a lot less common. It's so uncommon, in fact, that I don't have a great name for it (although, in retrospect, it turns up in analysis projects a surprising amount of the time).

The idea behind deep navigation is to identify sessions in which visitors were thrashing around and try to piece together clues about what they were looking for from the order of content they viewed, to the combinations of content, to the use of internal search. What defines "thrashing around?" Good question. We don't have one answer, of course, and every digital property is different. Typically, though, thrashing sessions last longer, consume more content, cross section boundaries, almost always involve some looping (anecdotally, we've all had that sinking feeling when we wind up back on a page we viewed 5 minutes ago as we try to find something), often involve internal search, usually have at least a couple high-linger-time pages, and almost never have any success events.

Looking at these thrashing sessions is a natural application of a customer experience management (CEM) tool, also called a session replay tool. CEM tools allow the analyst to follow along on any given session and see exactly what the user saw. The biggest challenge to using CEM tools is that it's hard to know which sessions to look at. Thrashing behaviors, however, are distinct enough to be selected in a CEM tool and re-created visually. It's not unreasonable to start with a simple definition of viewing a lot of pages and not having any success events. (Don't go for outliers: You don't want sessions with 300 page views that are almost certainly special cases—you want sessions with maybe 20 to 30 page views.) Try adding some of the other criteria, if necessary, as your tool supports.

Notice that this isn't a very scientific way of proceeding: It relies on session replay and the analyst's intuition to make sense of what the behavior means. That's not a criticism—just a reality. This method can work, but it's not a methodology with a formal set of processes behind it.

The last method for getting at selection limitation problems is voice of customer. The VoC space has at least three relevant methods. Most sites now have some direct feedback mechanism (comment cards) through which visitors can communicate issues, problems, suggestions, and even compliments. Users who generate comments are by no means a representative sample of your digital population. You can't use comment cards to understand demographics, measure brand attitudes, or do conjoint analysis of product features.

But don't discard a group of users who fill out a comment card because they most likely had problems. These users provide a potentially great way to discover selection limitation problems. As with the internal search box, comment cards are open ended. Users tell you what problems they had with essentially no guidance. Comments such as "I was looking for..." or "I couldn't find..." are fantastic for finding selection limitations.

Comment cards work precisely because they are an unguided "push" mechanism that users are particularly likely to turn to when they can't get what they need. However, you can also use traditional intercept (pop-up) surveys to try to understand selection limitations. Intercept surveys are a different beast from comment cards. Typically triggered on a random basis, intercept surveys are specifically intended to create a valid sample of your digital population and are meant to draw inferences about the population as a whole.

Intercept surveys are harder to use in this context because they typically reach only a small percentage of people. Unless your organization is unusually myopic, selection limitation gaps are limited to smaller groups of the digital population, and it's easier to miss them with intercept surveys. Intercept surveys also tend to ask closed-end questions in which the respondent chooses from a list or set of answers instead of offering free-form, open-ended feedback. Fortunately, nothing prevents you from using open-ended questions on a survey and even exploring selection limitations quite explicitly by asking questions of this sort: Was there anything you couldn't find? As you'll see in the next two chapters, one enormous advantage to using both comment cards and intercept surveys is that you can match the VoC responses to the site behavior, making it possible to understand where people looked when they couldn't find something.

Lastly, it's possible to use social media to research and understand selection limitations. Countless technology vendors and agencies tout the utility of social media for solving your marketing, brand, customer support, and research problems. Occasionally, it can even work.

Problems in sampling within social media make it challenging to use as a channel for traditional research or brand tracking. Although social media is often used in these contexts, the results aren't usually pretty. If you're in discovery mode around selection limitation problems and you're trying to discover what content you might be missing, social media is much more practical. As with comment cards, social media tends to surface more motivated outliers. That makes it perfect for this kind of work, when there's no assumption that you're tracking a representative sample of the digital population.

Also as with comment cards, social media is unguided. You aren't specifying the range of responses, and you're being exposed to natural, unsolicited commentary. For this particular problem set, that's good.

Two potential disadvantages of social media are worth mentioning. First, the quantity and quality of social media discourse varies wildly by company, industry, and problem. Some topics get a lot of social traction; others don't. You can't manufacture social content, and you can't research it when it doesn't exist in substantial volume. The first step in any social media research project is ascertaining the amount of actual content generated by relevant populations.

The second problem with social media is that it is even less guided than comment cards; the vast majority of chatter will likely be entirely irrelevant. Important issues on product selection or decision making also might never be discussed even when products are frequently mentioned. Social media is rarely a deep research vehicle, at least when it comes to commercial enterprises. People might say a great deal about politics or sports, but most people just don't post enough content about a product to be interesting.

Comment cards, intercept surveys, and social media all fill an important role in understanding the digital world. It's a role we dive into in great detail in coming chapters. As tools for discovering problems in selection limitation, each has a distinct and potentially useful niche.

Behavioral Shifting

If the analytics challenge to selection limitation is that we have no behavior to tell us what's missing, the challenge raised by behavioral shifting via site structure is that we have too much behavior. Virtually every action in the digital world reflects some balance between what the user intends and what content was offered. It's like a magic act between two magicians, each trying to force cards on the other. In such a situation, it's difficult to decide which of the two factors is dominant or what the relationship is between them.

Why does it matter?

Behavioral shifting matters because it reduces our ability to measure the two most important aspects of understanding the digital world. Because our understanding of what a visitor intended is driven by the choice of what to consume, a strong site structure constantly puts us in danger of misreading visitor intention. Then within a use case, we have to decide whether content is working because it expresses visitor intentions (as with the Open an Account link) or because it's actually shifting them. This is particularly important because sites don't just have structure in the way that, for example, a crystal has a structure or the roads of a city have structure. Website structures are expressly built to shift behaviors. Yes, similar to roads, they provide the pathways visitors traverse to arrive at a destination or continue to a journey. But unlike roads, in which size is nearly always a function of the traffic load they must carry, web elements are sized and placed with a strong eye to shifting behavior. More often than not, an element is placed top-of-fold on the home page with a big image because it's what you want people to click.

So when people click more on that big image than any other part of the home page, it's hard to know whether it's what they really wanted to do, whether the size of the image caused more people to click than otherwise would have, and whether the specific image did better than something else similarly sized would have done. Those are all critical points to understand if you really want to measure the digital world.

A long time ago, when I was a student of philosophy, a professor remarked that if someone gives three arguments for something, it probably means that none is very convincing. When an argument is truly convincing, you need only one. That's probably why, once again, I provide alternative techniques for dealing with behavioral shifting.

No single one is completely satisfactory or universally applicable. And although my professor's remark stuck with me and I have found it always true when reading philosophy, in the workaday world, it's rare to find a single solution to any complex problem. The world is hard. The digital world is hard. Sometimes you just have to use multiple arguments.

Controlled Experimentation

The problem of behavioral shifting has one nearly perfect type of answer. With controlled experiments (often called A/B tests or just tests), random site populations are served two different versions of the site. The difference between the two versions is often singular and highly specific—replacing a single image; changing its size, replacing one line or paragraph of content with another; changing the color, shape, or size of a page element; and so on.

When you change a single element in an experience and measure the impact on behavior with two random populations, you can provide fairly definitive answers to the types of behavioral shifting questions laid out earlier. If you shrink the size of a callout on the page and measure the difference in clicks between the large and small versions, you have a definitive measure of the impact of the size of the callout on visitor choice.

That's an important concept to absorb. A great deal of testing gets done in the digital world that means next to nothing. A designer picks two different images and runs a test. One works slightly better, so that's the image that gets used. This type of test isn't completely useless. After all, it improved site performance ever so slightly. What the designer learned, however, is completely singular. If he or she selected any other image, would it be better or worse than the one that just won (the "hero," in texting lingo)? There's no way to know.

Since an infinite number of possible images, alternative texts, and potential page layouts might work, testing specific instances only helps a designer resolve some internal choice. For it to be fruitful, you must assume that the designer has already narrowed the infinite set of choices to a couple good ones, and the test picks out the best of a select lot. But of course, when you've made that assumption, it would be quite surprising if either alternative significantly outperformed the other. Indeed, if that happened, you'd probably wonder whether you had a good designer. It's not surprising, therefore, that tests such as this rarely yield significant improvement. Mostly they return "no significance" answers; even when they do return a hero, the gain is trivial.

On the other hand, when you create a test that emphasizes the path to one use case versus another, you're creating a controlled experiment that measures something quite generalizable, interesting, and useful. You're not testing a specific creative element—you're measuring the elasticity of demand for a use case.

Economists use price elasticity to understand how markets react to changes. Some goods and services are fairly inelastic; substantial changes in price don't impact demand. Other types of products are just the reverse: Even a small change in price significantly impacts demand. The digital world has no corresponding concept of supply elasticity (content development), but it most certainly has one of demand (content consumption). It also encapsulates some of the same factors that determine price elasticity in markets.

Three factors drive use case elasticity: the degree to which the visitor is committed to a specific task, the degree to which the visitor wants to do the task right now, and the degree to which that task is unique to a digital property.

Going back to an earlier example with a brokerage site, visitors might visit the trading site intending to buy a specific stock. The intensity of that desire can vary (although it's often pretty strong when it reaches the level of visiting with intent to buy), as can the intensity of the desire to do it *now*. If long-term considerations shape the intention, it's much more likely that the visitor will switch to a different task or buy a different stock than if immediate considerations such as breaking news shape the intention. For a trading site, it's quite unlikely that the visitor will switch sites. People don't open a new (additional) brokerage account to buy a single stock.

Suppose, on the other hand, that you hear about a breaking news story and visit a news site. If your desire to find this story is strong, you might be unlikely to first consume other content on the site. However, if you don't see the story or can't easily find it with search, your ability to switch sites and consume the content elsewhere is high.

One aspect that really differentiates the digital world from the physical world is the remarkably low friction involved in traveling between properties. In the physical world, going from a Home Depot to a Lowes, for example, often involves significant hassle. Given the travel cost, visitors accept a certain amount of additional cost or product desirability to avoid visiting multiple locations. In the digital realm, that's much less likely. Because the friction of travel in the physical world drives many merchandising and pricing strategies (it's why, for example, grocery stores offer huge discounts on turkey right before Thanksgiving—they know you're likely to fill your cart with other items, too), it's dangerous to think that similar strategies will work in the digital realm.

The demand elasticity for a use case is also a function of the specific trade-off the user is asked to make. Some use cases are more related, and it's easier to shift the user between them. Suppose, for example, that you come to a news website intending to check the Giants baseball score. You'll more likely shift into an article about Tim Lincecum (one-time Giants wunderkind) than to an article about the real estate market. Understanding which use cases are related can help a designer figure out which links and drives should go where inside the digital property.

Understanding the elasticity of demand for the use cases on a digital property is essential to making decisions about how the site should lay out, which content paths should get the most real estate, which need to be clearly accessible (to keep visitors from switching to other properties), and where on the site it's worth trying to significantly shift consumption behavior. In short, almost every major decision about site real estate, navigation, and offer strategy should be driven by an understanding of the demand elasticity for each use case, as well as the ways in which use cases are related.

So after you've developed your use cases analytically, the logical next step is a set of controlled experiments to measure how focused visitors are on that use case when they arrive at the site, how much you can shift their behavior by tweaking the site structure, and which use cases are most strongly related.

Controlled experiments designed to achieve this generate real knowledge. The learnings can apply across a huge range of design and optimization decisions and help make sense of the actual measurement on a digital property.

This line of discussion might suggest that the principle use or only use of controlled experimentation is to understand the elasticity of use cases and help build the measurement foundation. That's not right. Controlled experiments are essential to building out a measurement foundation, fleshing it out beyond a bare-bones segmentation into a broader understanding of how visitors use a digital property.

However, the utility of controlled experiments doesn't stop there. Controlled experiments remain the most powerful tool in the analyst's arsenal for resolving thorny measurement issues where the impacts of self-selection, structure, and shifting are too complex to sort out.

Consider another example of how a disciplined approach to controlled experimentation can drive measurement answers that would be challenging or impossible otherwise. With the explosion in bandwidth, video has become an increasingly popular way to deliver content online. Naturally, many existing digital properties (ecommerce sites, financial services sites, life science sites, news publishers, and more) are interested in adding video content.

Typically, an enterprise goes about this by developing one or a small number of video assets and then deploying them on the digital property. Perhaps they create a welcome video for the home page, a product video for one product, and a user video on the customer support page.

Ideally, using analytics, we should be able to answer all the following questions:

- Does adding video improve site performance?
- Where does adding video have the biggest impact?
- Where should videos be located on the page?
- Should videos be autoplay or user started?
- What's the ideal length of a video?
- What's the impact of different video quality on performance?

Given our measurement foundation, there's a good chance we'll be able to answer the first question (whether adding video improves performance) without any controlled experimentation. If we're tracking use case and use case performance, then comparing the distribution of use cases and performance before and after adding video should provide a pretty clear answer.

Having said this, remember that before-and-after tests of this type are never quite as good as a true controlled experiment. When you do a before-and-after analysis, there's an implicit assumption that everything else is equal, as economists and statisticians like to say. (*Ceteris paribus* is the Latinate term social scientists love to use.) Unfortunately, things rarely are *ceteris paribus* for long in the digital world. Even if you haven't changed campaigns, altered or added content, changed prices, or had any of your competitors do these things, new factors arise: Time has passed, school might be a week closer, the weather might be different, the stock market might have gone up— the world might have changed in some significant way.

None of this means that before-and-after analysis isn't worthwhile. It's vitally important and it routinely works. It just carries an extra measure of risk that a true controlled experiment eliminates.

Likewise, we might take a stab at answering the question of where adding video has the biggest impact. The easy answer is to suggest that the use case with the greatest lift from video is the right answer. It's tricky, though, and it shouldn't be hard to understand why. Let's say that I add Michael Jordan (the greatest basketball player ever) as the shooting guard to the Bulls. Then I add Bill Cartwright (a decent center) to the same team. If I measure performance before and after, I'm sure to find that adding a two-guard made more difference than adding a center. But the conclusion is driven by the player, not the position. If I have only one video in each section, it's pretty much impossible to decide analytically whether the difference in performance is because one video was better than another or because one location is a better place for a video.

This same theme repeats when we try to answer the other questions. If a video at the top of the page is performing better than a video at the bottom of the page, it could be because that's a better location for a video. Or it could be because that video is better. It could also be because that type of content is a better fit for video. Each factor we consider further complicates the analysis, making it impossible to separate out any single impact.

We can tackle these problems and separate out impacts in certain ways. For example, we can measure the percentage of visitors who started the video at the top of the page and measure the percentage who started the video at the bottom. But even here, users in different use cases might be more or less likely to start videos, regardless of their location.

The simple fact is that analysis works against variation. In many cases, plenty of variation exists in the world (digital or otherwise) and you don't have to create controlled experiments to isolate it. If you want to understand the impact of temperature on cookie purchases at a Mrs. Fields store, you can take advantage of the natural variation in temperatures to build a pretty good guess.

When you have only a few elements, however, you simply don't have enough natural variation to analyze. Digital properties routinely make the mistake of trying functionality in a way that's too limited to allow for actual measurement.

Of course, you can just wait a few years until video is everywhere on the website and in all sorts of forms, and you'll have the raw material for analysis. But perhaps it makes more sense to create variation intentionally. That's what a controlled experiment does. By first thinking of the questions you need to answer and then trying each variation systematically (for example, you try the same video in each use case at the top and bottom of the page, you try different length videos in each use case and in each position, and so on), you can answer the questions about performance, placement, length, autoplay, and more once and for all, in a way that lets designers take advantage of the answers over and over again.

Controlled experimentation is a good answer to the problems of self-selection, structure, and behavioral shifting. It solves them all well. It's not the only answer you need, though. Many types of problems are expensive or difficult to test experimentally.

Mixing Your Own Experiments

Controlled experimentation of the purposeful sort described earlier (which is rarer than iridium in testing practices out there) is the gold standard when it comes to providing definitive answers to measurement questions—and that's as true in the physical world as it is in the digital world. But just as some problems in the physical world don't lend themselves to easy experimentation (think evolution, stellar evolution, and string theory), many problems in the digital world are either too expensive or too difficult to test. If you want to know whether a video works better at the top of a page or the bottom, it's easy to test it. But if a test involves building a lot of new creative, fundamentally changing the site structure, and changing prices or product features, or if it impacts small populations that would be hard to measure for significance, then a true controlled experiment could cost a lot in terms of money and time.

Behind nearly every analytic problem in the digital world lies the problem of deciding which of two (or more) approaches works better. It might be a navigation path, a campaign, a piece of content, a complete experience, an app, or a website—it almost doesn't matter. In almost every case, it's easy to see which option works better based on the key metrics for the business: consumption, conversion, profit, or satisfaction. Yet every measurement is potentially undercut by the questions of structure, self-selection, and behavioral shifting. Is the winner better, or is it just the natural path? Does it benefit by having a better audience? Is it a path you forced on the user?

Part of the difficult job of analysis is to get the best possible answer to the question of which works better. And the best possible answer is almost never the simple, immediate measurement of KPIs.

To get a better answer, you should try to approximate what would happen in a controlled experiment. From an analytics perspective, this means holding as many key variables constant as possible when measuring the two experiences. This is an exercise in segmentation.

Which variables count as "key?"

There's no way to know for sure which variables need to stay constant to achieve the best result. Perhaps even more frustrating, there's no way to decide that you got the right answer and picked the right variables (except by running a controlled experiment). That doesn't make the exercise either pointless or impossible; it just makes it real.

If you don't have any absolute answers to what variables you need to hold constant to approximate a controlled experiment, some pretty good ones nearly always help. At a high level, the goal is to control for the type, the qualification level, and the pre-behavior of each visitor consuming the experience.

As a first step, hold constant the sourcing to each experience when you measure each alternative. The quality of visitors from various campaigns and channels is notoriously different. By looking at the performance for direct visitors, PPC visitors, SEO visitors, display visitors, and so on for each experience, you can eliminate many biases caused by differences in the quality of audience marketing programs drive to each alternative.

Next, hold constant and compare the type of visitors at the deepest reasonable level. If it's possible to identify the difference between customers and prospects, it's essential to use that segmentation in the comparison. At a minimum, holding the measurement constant by visit number helps distinguish between performance driven by new versus repeat visitors.

If the experience is deeper on a digital property, holding the entry page constant can make for an interesting comparison. Often this is driven by source, but entry page can be significant as an indicator of initial concern. By controlling for it, you can eliminate some significant selection biases.

Finally, it's important to control for the behavior that happened before the two alternatives. If one experience is typically consumed after a visitor has read 20 pages and the other experience comes into play after a visitor has read 2 pages, then performance differences likely are driven by the breadth of prior experience, not the two alternatives.

Ideally, you want to compare a set of populations held constant for marketing source, visitor type, and several common variations of site experience. If a comparison is limited to visitors who sourced in the same channel, have the same number of prior visits, are generally the same class of customer, and viewed exactly the same content earlier, then the control group is strong.

Of course, just as it's often impossible to run every controlled experiment that might be desirable, it's often impossible to get enough behavior to create such a detailed set of control groups. Do the best job possible. If it's impossible to control for campaign because all the behavior for an experience is sourced by a single campaign, try to control for visitor type and prior experience. If you don't have visitor type information, try to control for prior behavior as richly as possible. There's a good chance that strict controls based on prior behavior will capture many biases caused by differences in customer type.

The profile report described earlier in the section on validating segmentation rules is an extremely valuable tool for helping mix good controlled experiments. That report makes it easy to see how two segments compare—and by creating segments that begin with the users of each alternative and then gradually adding control conditions, you should see the profiles gradually converge. However, to make this report ideal for mixing controlled experiments, the behavior profiling should be split into a before-and-after profile based on when the behavior occurs.

In other words, the ideal control group doesn't have identical total behavior (before and after the two experiences)—it has identical prior behavior. By building a report that profiles prior behavior and post behavior, it's easy to quickly measure both the precision of the control groupings (in the degree to which the prior behavior matches) and get a snapshot of performance (in the behavior after the two alternatives).

The process of mixing a controlled experiment is salutary in every respect. Not only does an analysis that uses a controlled experiment deliver far more thoughtful and accurate answers, but it forces the analyst to address both the risks and the limitations of the analysis. By putting front and center the question of what is needed to create a good control, the analyst is driven to take better account of the structural and self-selection forces that drive so much digital behavior.

The relationship between experimentation and analysis is poorly understood by most practitioners of each discipline. Controlled experimentation provides definitive answers but lacks any method of identifying the right questions. It can be expensive, intrusive, and cumbersome. Analysis is great for identifying the key questions and suggesting possible answers, and analysis doesn't impact the user experience. But analysis is often stymied by lack of variation and lack of control. Techniques like mixing your own experiments can help, yet there's never a guarantee you've found the right answer. By bringing the two together and understanding how and when each works best, it's possible to tackle the formidable challenges from self-selection and structure that lie at the very heart of measuring the digital world.

6

Attitudes and Behaviors: Mixing a More Powerful Measurement Cocktail

Two-tiered segmentation and site topology create a powerful, robust framework for measuring behavior. By understanding and interpreting what content visitors consume, it's possible to gain a much deeper understanding of what they were trying to accomplish in your digital world and whether or not they were successful. As powerful as this is, however, it's still missing some important points. Knowing what people do rarely tells us why they took the paths they did or what attitudes drove critical decisions about where to go and whether to continue with a digital interaction. In this chapter, we look at how you can integrate voice of customer (VoC) research with behavioral data to construct a better, richer, more accurate behavioral segmentation.

Two-tiered segmentation provides a truly robust foundation for measuring the digital world. When supplemented by understanding the ways self-selection and structural biases create behavioral shifting, it can explicate a huge amount of digital behavior. There are limits, however, to the depth that any purely behavioral segmentation can provide. Those limits aren't fixed or certain. They depend on the type of digital property in question and the behavioral patterns of a specific user. Because some visitors demonstrate far more behavior, they can be understood in more depth and with more certainty. Nor are all behaviors created equal. Some behaviors (such as carting, seeking customer support, or reading the jobs page) are simply more revealing than others (such as landing on a home page). Even where the amount of demonstrated behavior is truly vast (think Netflix, Amazon, or Facebook), much that is potentially interesting can't be inferred from behavior alone. When the amount of information is dramatically more limited, as it is for most digital properties, site behaviors sometimes open only the narrowest of windows into the nature, interests, and decision-making process of a site's users.

Fortunately, a readily available technique can extend our range of knowledge about digital behavior and both improve and help validate a purely behavioral understanding of the digital world. Long before the advent of digital worlds, researchers and analysts used survey research to segment, profile, and understand different populations. From politics, to brand awareness, to product research, one of the most effective techniques for understanding people has always been to ask them what they think.

In the digital world, asking people what they think is easy. Indeed, it's so easy and inexpensive that it's hard not to overindulge in the practice, to the point of annoying your customers. This type of research is called voice of customer (VoC). As previously discussed, three major types of VoC take place in the digital realm: online surveys, comment cards, and unguided social media research. All three methods are useful and serve different purposes. For building segmentations and supplementing a behavioral measurement framework, online surveys are uniquely important.

Online surveys offer some significant advantages when it comes to creating a digital measurement framework. Unlike comment cards, online surveys are designed to capture representative samples of users. That makes them far more valuable when it comes to broader analytic purposes, particularly if you need to use statistical methods to analyze the data. In addition, online surveys are guided. The survey instrument can be structured to answer specific questions about the customer journey and how that journey can be translated into a segmentation. Both comment cards and social media are unguided, so they rarely provide insight into key journey steps or the decisions that drove them. And although these techniques might expose customer attitudes and concerns that you didn't otherwise imagine, they almost never allow for deep insight into any specific questions.

Online surveys (also called pop-up and intercept surveys) can be highly customized in terms of when and to whom they are delivered and the nature of the survey instrument itself. Surveys range from a single question to many hundreds of questions, and question types can run the gamut from multiple-choice questions, to scalar ratings, to open-ended questions and everything in between. In addition, surveys can target almost any population of users on a digital property. The survey ask can be executed on entry, on exit, on arrival at a specific page, or after some basic set of criteria is met (such as time on property or number of pages consumed). The tremendous flexibility on the time and nature of the ask make online surveys powerful and useful in a huge variety of digital research applications.

For the purposes of building a measurement foundation, online surveys are useful in four ways: to understand site behavior and set the table for designing a behavioral segmentation, to "color" a segmentation and more easily understand users and their intent, to validate a segmentation by showing that the behavioral filters match stated visit intents and self-reported success, and to build a segmentation by providing a set of target variables that can be used to create behavioral signatures.

Understanding Site Behavior

Two basic approaches work when creating a segmentation. A bottom-up, data-driven approach uses clustering techniques to create segments driven by similar patterns of consumption. A top-down approach relies on the analyst to describe segments and then create rules that match those segments as well as possible. For a top-down approach, one of the key questions is where those visit type segments come from. Chapter 3, "Use Cases and Visit Intent," cited the site design specification (which is often use case driven) and a site walk-through as potential starting points for a solution. Those methods both work, but doesn't it make more sense to ask your visitors what they are using the digital property for? The single most basic question (and one of the most useful) in digital VoC research is, why are you here? This visit intent question is a natural starting point for a top-down segmentation.

Those familiar with the common survey wording of the visit intent question might object that it's most often presented as a list of choices. This can be helpful in understanding the distribution of visit types, but presenting a closed list of choices requires that the relevant visit types already be identified. Fortunately, visit intent doesn't have to be presented as a closed list of choices.

In fact, for most questions in which you're giving the respondent a closed list of choices, it's not a bad idea to occasionally test an open-ended version of the question instead. Most survey tools support "tests" of alternative questions. Carving out a random group of respondents and asking them an open-ended version of the "Why are you here?" question makes it fairly easy to compare the responses and the distribution of responses between the open-ended version and a list of choices.

If you're really bootstrapping a problem, you can start with an open-ended question, classify the responses, test a list selection, and then make sure that the distribution of responses to the list selection matches fairly closely to the distribution of responses based on the original classification. This method provides a full open-ended exploration of why people visit a digital property, along with a disciplined approach to making sure that your classification of open-ended responses isn't significantly shifting the way people answer the question.

Longer term, and for analytics, there's good reason to prefer the list-of-choices question: It's much easier to use and analyze. But starting with and occasionally testing an open-ended variation can ensure that you've covered the right bases and kept the potential responses fresh and comprehensive.

An open-ended visit intent question (or a closed list that's been validated) can easily form the starting point of a behavioral segmentation. Not only is this a more data-driven approach to a top-down segmentation, but it also provides a deeper way to begin mapping the possible behavioral signatures for a segmentation.

A critical step in building the technology infrastructure for good digital measurement is integrating online survey data into the underlying behavioral data stream. This is usually a simple integration (if it isn't, fire your tools) in which the survey's respondent ID is passed into a variable in the digital analytics tracking. Then the survey responses are externally matched to the digital behavior using the respondent ID as the lookup value.

The beauty of this integration is that it links survey responses to digital behavior. Using the survey responses to filter a report, the analyst can see which consumption patterns are common for visitors who chose each response to the "Why are you here?" question.

For a top-down segmentation, there's no better starting place than this type of visit intent–to–site behavior reporting.

Coloring a Segmentation

This brings me to a huge pet peeve. True, many analysts focus too much on behavioral analysis and don't spend enough time thinking about VoC research. But if this is an occasional blind spot for analysts, it's much worse when it comes to the creative folks who design digital properties. Any good designer should insist on seeing deep survey research before starting a significant digital design project. It's just not possible to do a good design job unless designers have done the work to understand who the audience is, what they care about, and what they respond to. It's surely not the designer's job to create, execute, or analyze those surveys. But if your designer isn't insisting on seeing that research, chances are, you have the wrong designer. Too often, analysts and creative folks treat each other as antagonists, not partners, and it works to the detriment of each. The analysis necessary to help creative folks do their job isn't the same as the analysis necessary to drive SEO or CRO, and it can't be treated as if it were. Handing designers a Google Analytics report won't give them what they need. Instead, they need to understand the segmentation framework you've built and the VoC data that colors it.

How does VoC data color a segmentation? With online surveys, you can gather an almost limitless amount of information. You can collect traditional demographics such as age, income, gender, and education. You can also get life stage data (marital status, number of children, profession), attitudinal data (brand sentiment, product favorability), preference data (by brand or product feature type), knowledge level, media consumption patterns, other interests, preferred contact mechanisms, self-described tendencies (risk taker, DIYer), and so much more. Deciding which data to go after is a high art and necessarily involves a blend of intuition, business savvy, and empathy on what consumers are willing to share.

Much of this data is golden for marketers and creative designers. We spend all our lives categorizing people by gender, age, and education, so if nothing else, we get pretty good at it. Giving a marketer these key demographics can help flesh out a creative approach.

That being said, there's a negative to using those core demographics. After all, these are just stereotypes, and marketers all too often make the mistake of using stereotypes and anecdotes ("Some of my best friends are...") instead of real data. So although you shouldn't discard demographics, it's often better to look for deeper measurements that get at the attitudes you really care about.

For example, many aspects of how a person approaches investing decisions undoubtedly are strongly correlated to age. That might make age a quick and attractive proxy for attitudes and a valuable piece of data to collect. However, if it's possible to get at the actual attitudes that matter (such as knowledge, risk aversion, and advice propensity), that's much better than having a correlated variable such as age. After all, correlation isn't 100 percent—mostly, it's not even close: Age might be strongly correlated to risk aversion and still be a bad predictor 1 out of 3 times.

By integrating the VoC data to the behavioral data, you can profile each behavioral segment by any of the VoC variables you collect. For a marketer, that means each use case can be described in terms of the demographics of its users, their brand preferences, their pre-existing attitudes about the enterprise, the degree of their knowledge about the products or services, and even the factors they care about most or use to decide on a course of action.

That's obviously critical information for anyone trying to build experiences or design creative material for those visitors. Remember that profile report the analyst can use to help build and validate segments? It's a good starting point for building a creative brief template for designers, testers, marketers, and site experience folks. Before you ship it, however, take the time to color it with a much richer and deeper set of VoC data points.

Validating Segmentations

Sometimes analytics seems to get a free pass from information consumers. As likely as not, an analysis is greeted with welcoming nods. After all, people are hungry for data and often keenly aware of all they don't know. Most analysis also tends to confirm points that people have long suspected. This isn't somehow a fault of analysis—it's just a testament to the fact that people often have a pretty decent idea of what's going on.

Other times, however, an analysis is greeted with attitudes hovering somewhere between skepticism and hostility. That can be the case especially if digital analysis is driving a fundamental change in the way the business works, whether in creative development or digital marketing spend. Of course, that's exactly what you should expect a good digital measurement foundation to do. It's a good idea to expect some resistance to a digital segmentation, and whether a segmentation is top down or bottom up, an analyst often must defend it.

How do you that?

You have internal defenses, of course. You can discuss and justify the logic of the segmentation, the behavioral profiles, and the analytic methods. However, none of this can really *prove* that a segmentation is valid.

On the other hand, with the combination of VoC data and segmentation, it's almost trivial to show how predictive the segmentation is in terms of self-reported categories of visitor and visit type. What's more, it's possible to explore areas in which the segmentation isn't predictive and show why certain groups of users might self-describe in ways contrary to their behavior.

By showing how a segmentation classifies each VoC respondent and then mapping that to the visitors' stated visit intent and task accomplishment, an analyst can demonstrate the accuracy of a segmentation and the resulting success criteria for that segmentation.

It's hard to argue with real numbers.

Nor is this just an effort in justification. If VoC data is available, analysts would be neglectful not to validate a segmentation by crosstabulating with the self-reported VoC data to ensure that the segmentation is indeed capturing what it intends. The earlier case in which stated visit intent and behavior don't match is a great example that's always worth investigating when doing this type of validation. A mismatch might indicate a segmentation issue, but it might also point to genuine site problems. Issues such as misleading link names, poor navigation, or too-strong structural shifting can all result in warps where stated intent and behavior mismatch.

No absolute threshold exists for calling a segmentation a success. Every segmentation problem is different. Some segments and some segmentations are distinct and crisp. Sometimes, however, reliably pulling apart one or more segments can be difficult. A VoC cross-tabulation shows how much fuzziness exists and where overlaps can be problematic. This might suggest a consolidation of multiple segments into a single group. If two segments can't be reliably differentiated with behavior, no matter how thorough the search for behavioral cues, it's better to just consolidate them than to keep them distinct while knowing that the behavioral assignment isn't reliable.

At the same time, no behavioral segmentation can be expected to achieve anything like 100 percent accuracy in a cross-tabulation with VoC data. This is prediction, not accounting, and a model that works well most of the time is good enough. What's more, assuming that VoC data is somehow a perfect gold standard is a mistake. Survey intercept data is imperfect for many reasons. Survey researchers know that the order of items in a list and small variations in phrasing can have significant impacts on response rates, especially in borderline situations. What's more, self-reported data always has a certain fuzziness to it. Because many analytics projects integrate self-reported and behavioral data, it's often possible to see places where self-reporting fails or has higher error rates than behavioral data. In one customer support analysis project, site search was one of the lowest-scoring functional components of a website in terms of satisfaction. However, a detailed analysis of respondents showed that almost a third of the visitors who gave site search the lowest scores had never actually used the search functionality. In matching with behavioral data, the expectation should always be a good match, with an understanding that errors in use case identification are likely to crop up in both the behavioral segmentation and the self-reported VoC data. If a segmentation is accurate 75 percent of the time or better, that's usually good enough.

Building a Segmentation

VoC is helpful in starting, coloring, and validating a segmentation, but in none of these cases is it fundamental to the segmentation itself. However, sometimes it makes sense to build a digital segmentation from the ground up with VoC data baked in. You can do this in two ways, each with some distinct advantages.

The first method for incorporating VoC into a behavioral segmentation is to restrict the analysis population to survey respondents and drive a bottom-up segmentation using a full combination of VoC data and digital behavior. With this method, demographic variables such as age, income, and gender live side by side with attitudinal variables such as visit intent and brand awareness, as well as behavioral variables such as page-type consumption, viewing behavior, and purchase behavior. This makes for a rich segmentation indeed and is particularly useful in clustering. With all the behavioral and VoC data points deployed, chances are good that the resulting segmentation will feature a rich, interesting blend of both types of data.

The big drawback to this approach is that the resulting segmentation doesn't apply to all visitors. If the segmentation is built with VoC data baked right into the clustering or decision trees, it won't be possible to categorize most visitors. After all, only a small fraction of visitors will respond to VoC surveys. For most visitors, the demographic and attitudinal variables just won't be available.

If the goal of a segmentation is simply to inform the business, then it's almost always a good idea to use *every* available data point that's potentially interesting. Naturally, that includes VoC data. On the other hand, if the goal of a segmentation is to drive reporting, further analysis, or targeting, then building rare or sparse data elements deeply into the segmentation defeats these purposes.

Because these uses are nearly always part of what a segmentation is intended for, baking the VoC data directly into the segmentation is pretty rare. However, another way of using the VoC data can open up some modeling approaches to segmentation building that would not otherwise be available. This approach can produce a better visit segmentation that still applies to the entire range of digital visitors.

The most common method of building customer segmentations is clustering. Several techniques are involved in clustering, but the general concept is that data is first standardized (so that, for example, all variables are expressed in terms of standard deviations) and then mapped across n dimensions, with each variable forming a separate dimension.

A traditional scatterplot is a good visualization of this for two variables (see Figure 6.1).

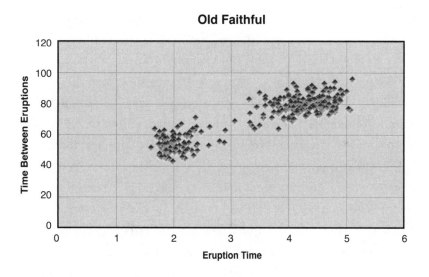

Figure 6.1 Old Faithful shows off her clustering

When the variables are mapped (in however many dimensions it takes), the data often forms clusters of points that map spatially together. Clustering algorithms are really just mathematical ways to draw lines around those clusters.

This type of approach to segmentation is purely data driven. Except for choosing the variables (which is a huge deal), the analyst makes no predetermination about the nature of the clusters. Unlike in a top-down segmentation, the results are entirely data driven, and that's generally considered good.

Clustering is a powerful and proven approach to segmentation. It's also the most common technique for building the type of behavioral segmentations described in the digital measurement foundation. However, clustering has a few drawbacks that sometimes merit considering an alternative approach that integrates VoC data more deeply and changes the nature of the analysis.

Three objections surface when using clustering as a segmentation technique for digital. First, clustering is a notoriously unstable analysis technique. Where you draw those lines and how they get drawn is a tricky problem—it's not unusual for clusters to disappear or warp when an analysis is repeated. Because the business builds marketing campaigns and reporting around a digital segmentation, that lack of stability can be troubling. The second problem is that although data-driven approaches appear to remove human direction, they often reintroduce it in a second step when the clusters are described. Keep in mind that a cluster analysis yields a set of equations that can be used to classify any data point in terms of its distance from the cluster center. The data point is said to belong to the cluster center it is closest to. But what cluster is that? You can't describe the cluster to the business in terms of an equation. In practical terms, after a clustering segmentation is created, the analyst typically runs something like a standard profile report (which is a huge tool for an analyst) and then names and describes the cluster in terms of the variables it tends to weight strongly in. This naming and descriptive process is critical to the success of the segmentation because it "sells" the segmentation and makes it useable. It's also a subjective exercise that reintroduces many analyst expectations that a data-driven approach was supposed to eliminate. Finally, clustering segmentations can be problematic because they don't always capture some of the key use cases the business is looking for. It's arguable how much of a problem this is. After all, the point of a data-driven segmentation is to identify what patterns actually exist, not what patterns the business *thinks* exist. It seems unfair (and sometimes is) to criticize a method because it refutes our expectations. Usually, though, the definition and description of clustered segmentations have enough vagary to be problematic if the segmentation appears to miss key use cases.

In any case, there's no point building a measurement foundation that won't be used. Depending on the nature of the organization and the interests involved, sometimes a measurement foundation either must capture some key elements of the users' intuitions or must have unassailable arguments for why it doesn't.

You can use VoC data to solve some of these problems. The earlier section "Understanding Site Behavior" described a two-step process for using VoC to nail down the types of visits users intend to have on a digital property. That method starts with an open-ended question to find all the likely reasons users visit the site; then it groups them and narrows them to a list selection that forces users to self-classify among the reasonably common choices. With this data in hand, it's possible to build a segmentation using only VoC respondents, but including both the behavioral data and the VoC data.

This sounds like our first approach, which limited the segmentation's use cases when we had VoC data. But instead of using all the VoC data, the idea is to use only the visit intent question. That question is the *target* of the segmentation.

In other words, the goal becomes to predict the VoC visit intent answer using the behavioral data.

The beauty of this approach is that, when that method is found, every visit can be classified, regardless of whether VoC data exists. What's more, this approach opens up a huge new set of analytic techniques beyond clustering. With a variable that can be used to determine the success of a prediction, the nature of the problem changes dramatically. The available methods are both more sustainable and more stable than in most clustering techniques. The VoC intent data nearly always matches business expectations reasonably well—and when it doesn't, it provides a strong justification back to the business on why there's a miss. It's hard to argue with your visitors.

Using VoC data to build the visit intent segmentation solves all three challenges common to clustering techniques. But—and this probably isn't too surprising—it has a few challenges of its own.

One potential issue with driving a segmentation around VoC visit intent data is how reliable that VoC data is. In effect, self-reported intent becomes the gold standard for building behavioral profiles that predict a visitor's stated intent. If it's not accurate, neither is the segmentation. It's easy to see how self-reported data on using internal search or buying a product might not be accurate, but it's less obvious how self-reported data on personal intent could be wrong. Who else would know?

Nevertheless, in some situations, self-reported intent is demonstrated to be wrong. In political elections, opinion researchers find that, for certain types of questions, people often self-report in a manner that doesn't reflect the way they actually vote. This happens most commonly when people perceive that there is a broad expectation that they will respond a certain way, even though privately they are inclined to disagree. This is not a common situation in most online research in the digital world.

But it's surprising how important and subtle these relationships can be. People might arrive at a site looking for information about a product but fully intending to buy it on Amazon. They might feel a little guilty about that if they are on a manufacturer's website with ecommerce enabled, and that might color their responses on visit intent.

Don't read too much into this. Shadow biases sometimes make self-reported intent unreliable, and although it's important to understand this class of problem, it's not likely to be a broad issue in digital measurement. Be aware, but there's no need to be paranoid.

The second issue with VoC-driven segmentation is more important and does need to be considered carefully before you embark on a VoC-driven segmentation. In the old world of traditional offline marketing, most segmentations had between four and eight groupings. That choice wasn't driven by the mathematics of clustering—it was mostly driven by the need to have a small enough number of segments for the business to understand and use effectively. It was also a function of the type and granularity of the demographic variables that drove most of that persona-based segmentation and the extent to which those variables could be refined when used for targeting. Particularly in the old-old world of three TV stations, targeting 25- to 27-year-olds was pointless. Every TV show distributed over a much broader range of values in the core demographics, so there wasn't much point in trying to identify microsegments even though the variables would have supported it.

Digital mostly doesn't work that way. Large, complex properties often have very fine-grained segmentations in both audience and visit intent that drive fundamental differences in the way the site is used and the corresponding measurements of success for those users. This is a challenge for VoC because capturing intent in VoC is difficult except in very broad-brush terms. You can't expect a survey respondent to choose from 50 options. Typically, list selection questions feature eight or fewer alternatives, or they simply become confusing. In other words, your segmentation will likely need to be much finer grained than your online survey self-reporting will support.

This problem does have work-arounds. Instead of thinking about a single tier of visit intent questions, you can structure your survey to have a top tier that encapsulates the broad uses of your digital property and then branches into subquestions that further refine the high-level segmentation into subcases.

It's even possible to combine the top-down and bottom-up approaches into a single segmentation scheme by using the high-level VoC data to create models that categorize users according to the VoC segments. Inside that, each visitor is then further categorized into subsegments using data-driven clustering techniques. Combining the methods is more work, but it preserves some of the virtues of each method.

Using and combining attitudinal data and behavioral data is exceptionally easy in digital measurement, and its value can hardly be overstated. Given that the foundation of digital measurement is determinedly behavioral, this isn't necessarily expected or obvious, and it's an area where practitioners' opinions can differ sharply. At one time, I classified myself as a VoC skeptic for measuring the digital world. Many of my reasons for skepticism are valid. Do we really want to duplicate the type of age/gender/income targeting that dominated old-world marketing? Probably not. But VoC doesn't necessarily mean relying on the tired old demographic stereotypes for high-level marketing personas. Exploring attitudes and behavior in conjunction opens up new types of questions and delivers answers that simply aren't achievable by either technique used in isolation. As you've seen in this chapter, VoC data can help shape and build a strong behavioral measurement foundation. Even though that foundation is fundamentally about measuring how people behave, what they say about their intent and behavior can be enormously useful. It can help an analyst lay out the basic structure of a top-down segmentation, it can help color a segmentation and make it useful to information consumers, it can validate and prove a segmentation's predictive power, and, perhaps most surprisingly, it can even aid in the statistical construction of the behavioral segmentation.

Survey Mechanics

A few basic blocking and tackling issues in online surveys can materially affect the success of a measurement program. If you're driving an online survey program, one of the first questions you'll be asked to answer is how many survey respondents you need. Let's say you get 100,000 visits in a month, and 1 in 20 respondents who are asked will complete a survey. If you want 1,000 completed surveys a month, you have to pop up a survey ask every fifth visit. The variables you have to work with are site traffic, response rate (and completion rate), and the target number of surveys. Assuming that site traffic is out of your control and response rate is largely fixed, the number of survey respondents you target is the key to setting a sampling rate.

How big of a sample do you need?

In one sense, you can immediately derive the answer to this question. Statisticians can tell you the confidence interval for any given research question if you know the sample size, the population, and the confidence level you want to achieve. What's more, you don't really need a big sample to answer any single question with a fairly high level of confidence.

Unfortunately, this easy approach to picking a sample doesn't actually work in practice. Analysts quickly discover that if they use this method for deciding on a sitewide sample, they mostly can't incorporate VoC data into their analysis. The problem is that, for most research questions, the sample size is only a small percentage of the entire survey population.

Consider our example of 100,000 site visits and 1,000 survey respondents. Now suppose that, instead of looking at all site visits, the analysis focuses on visits that included an internal search using the VoC data matched to the behavioral data. If 10 percent of all site visits use internal search, then we can expect to have only about 100 visits a month that had an internal search *and* a survey response. One hundred survey responses is already too small to generate a confident prediction to most questions, but the problems just get worse. Suppose that, in addition to internal search, we're focused on a single customer support use case that makes up about 30 percent of internal search usage. With this additional requirement, we'd expect only about 30 survey respondents per month that conducted an internal search for customer support and had a survey response. That's too few respondents to ever derive a statistically significant answer.

The more cuts you want to do on the data and the finer grained those cuts are, the larger the sample you need to generate good answers. In lieu of a fixed research program, a "correct" or "sufficient" sample doesn't exist. Unless you know all the ways the data will be used, there's no way to know whether a sample size is anywhere near large enough.

Between the very large site volumes that are common in the digital world and the ubiquitous use of segmentation as part of the measurement foundation, it's common to be analyzing small subpopulations that are no more than 1 or 2 percent of the total behavior pool. To integrate VoC data into those analytics projects, the sample size must be large enough to support at least two cross-tabulations of VoC data within 1 percent of the behavioral population. That's a much, much larger sample size.

When analysts start to ask for bigger samples, however, online research programs often face pushback. Site experience professionals don't like to disrupt the user experience with online research, and what these pros might tolerate for every hundredth session could seem counterproductive when asked for every other session.

This isn't unreasonable. Unlike behavioral measurement, there really is a trade-off between user experience and analytics when it comes to VoC.

You can avoid or mitigate this risk in three ways when building a survey program. The first method is to improve response rates. The better the response rate, the less often you need to ask. Response rates differ for every brand and also change globally over time. However, most sites can improve response rates by testing the language and placement of the ask and shortening the survey (shorter surveys also produce better completion rates).

Another strategy is to focus the ask in specific situations and use customized surveys for research. By targeting a survey specifically to the target population, the sample no longer needs to be segmented. In the previous example, a survey ask that pops up only for users of internal search would have the initial segmentation baked into the survey response population.

Finally, it's important to realize that surveys are part of the user experience. Making surveys visually more attractive, making the questions more interesting, and introducing gamification concepts (in short, creating surveys that enhance the user experience instead of destroying it) can make survey participation a positive part of the digital world.

Building good online survey instruments is an art, but keeping a few simple rules in mind definitely helps. The shorter the survey, the better the take-up rate (if the ask takes advantage of the brevity) and the higher the completion rate. Never ask for more than you need. Ask only questions that are relevant and interesting to the target population—use branching. Don't ask questions you already know the answer to (and can get simply by matching data sources). Finally, don't be afraid to make a survey fun.

The better the blocking and tackling on the survey mechanics is, the more surveys you can afford to collect and deploy. That's a key part of building a VoC program dedicated to understanding the digital world.

7

Voice of Customer, Digital Marketing, and Success Measurement

When we ask for someone's opinion, we get a snapshot in time of what that person thinks. Online surveys (and digital visits) are the same. To really understand someone, you need more than a snapshot. You need to be able to understand how that person's opinions evolve over time and how his or her behaviors are driven by and, in turn, shape those opinions. You can create a research program that helps you do that. In this chapter, we focus on extending voice of customer (VoC) research to understand visitors' attitudes and state across their digital journey.

The last chapter focused on the role of VoC analytics in developing and deploying the segmentation at the core of digital measurement. Although that core is fundamentally about measuring behavior to understand customers, the value of asking people who they are, what they are about, and why they are doing it is clear. Nevertheless, it's possible and even common to build a digital measurement framework on a purely behavioral basis. Incorporating VoC is kind of like using a seatbelt: You really should do it, and it'll get you where you want to go more safely, but it's not absolutely essential. With other fundamentally important types of digital measurement, however, VoC isn't optional, but lives at the core of a digital analytics strategy.

In many respects, the point of two-tiered segmentation is to understand the customer journey. For a journey-based analysis, however, it can feel more like a set of snapshots than a moving picture. The two-tiered segmentation captures the intent of a visitor at each visit or unit-of-work. By stringing together those visit type segmentation codes, it's possible to build a reasonable picture of a visitor's digital experience. But even with the best possible digital segmentation, this picture is usually missing two important aspects of the journey. With most digital segmentations, it's hard to understand the arrival state of visitors as a use case. Sometimes use cases are specifically constructed to separate users based on their journey stage (splitting early-stage shoppers from serious buyers, for example). Even when that's the case, though, visitors within the same journey stage usually differ greatly in their level of qualification. Not all serious buyers are equally serious, and not all early-stage shoppers have the same potential for conversion. In other words, the journey stage is an important part of understanding a visitor's qualification level, but it's far from the only factor involved; qualification exists independently of journey stage. It would be nice to understand differences in qualification level within each use case so that the effectiveness of a digital property can be measured consistently even when the distribution of qualified visitors changes.

If qualification is a significant miss in the existing digital measurement framework, the lack of insight into what happens outside the digital world is an even bigger miss. It sounds paradoxical to criticize a framework for measuring the digital world because it doesn't account for what happens outside that world. It isn't. The goal of our framework isn't to measure TV effectiveness, sales rep performance, or store sales. Measuring and understanding these non-digital channels requires specialized types of measurement. However, we can often understand the success of digital behaviors only when those digital behaviors are linked to outside actions.

Digital properties mostly don't exist as independent, completely contained worlds. Some do, but for most digital properties, important interactions take place between things that exist in the physical world (stores, branches, salespeople, call centers, and more).

Let's look at a bunch of examples to see what's at stake.

Digital Website to Retail Location

Pure-play ecommerce sites don't have to worry much about this, but for most retailers, sales come from both online ecommerce and in-store sales. The ecommerce part of the digital world is easy to measure and optimize for, and the two-tiered segmentation provides everything necessary to do that well. However, in an omnichannel world, the function of the digital property isn't just ecommerce. A significant percentage of visitors come to the digital property to research products but fully expect to shop in-store. This presents two challenges to the digital analyst. First, separating out those store shoppers from online buyers is hard. Almost by definition, store shoppers fail if the measurement of success is an ecommerce transaction. But suppose you could separate out store shoppers into their own use case? This would still leave a huge gap: measuring the success of those visits. You would have no way to decide which digital content actually helped drive store sales, so you would have little ability to measure success and even less to optimize the digital use cases designed to support in-store sales.

Acquisition Online and via Call Center

In many situations, customers can convert online or via a call center. Many "service" sells work this way because no physical pickup is involved. Plenty of businesses have evolved robust, phone-based business models that handle many, if not most, transactions. What's more, some kinds of transactions have a high degree of complexity and are difficult to navigate online (life insurance is a good example). When conversion can happen online or via call, optimizing the digital channel can be difficult. The problem is that the digital channel nearly always refers significant traffic to the call center. You aren't going to have a digital property without giving visitors the option to call and presenting a phone number for them to use. Unfortunately, you can't always track which visitors to the digital property ended up calling using those phone numbers. Of course, call tracking and dynamic phone number solutions help track how much volume in the call center a digital property or campaign generates. These are good solutions and an important part of effective digital measurement. But they don't solve the optimization problem of knowing which content on the digital property helps drive phone conversion. To get around this problem, analysts often assume that the content that works to drive online conversion is the same as the content that works to drive phone conversion. Ditto for digital campaigns. Those are dangerous assumptions to make. The online converting population is by no means a representative sample of the call center population, and there are often strong reasons to believe that performance in one channel will not mirror performance in the other. Where call centers are significant, therefore, it can be almost impossible to accurately measure the true success of either campaigns or content. And as we all know, what you can't measure, you can't optimize.

Online Broadcast and Show Consumption

The first two examples of online to offline are both commerce related, but the need for offline measurement is even more prevalent outside commerce. In broadcast, for example, a digital property is usually designed to support immediate viewership (digital streaming) and provide support in the form of engaging content that increases viewership in both online and offline channels. Streaming viewership is easily measured, and the entire digital experience can be optimized for streaming. Optimizing only for streaming, however, necessarily reduces or eliminates some content or navigation paths that might provide strong show support and lead to more offline viewing. In a site optimized purely for digital streaming, it would probably be a mistake to ever display the broadcast time of a show. That can't be optimal for the business, but it can certainly be optimal for a digital-only set of measurements.

Online Lead Generation and Sales Conversion

A huge range of B2B sites primarily are intended to support a broader sales process driven by actual salesmen. Typically, those sites provide a lot of content designed to interest potential buyers, give them product and feature information, support favorable comparisons with competitors' products, and possibly drive to online leads. The drive to online leads is the simple and easy part of measuring a B2B site. Everything else gets complicated and requires effectively measuring offline integration. If you can't tell which online consumption drives to offline lead conversion, which marketing programs drive the most qualified leads, and which types of experiences are most effective for each type of company, you can't really measure a B2B site. But all that information necessarily exists outside the digital world.

Product Support with Commerce Elsewhere Online or Offline

Companies that sell through other channels face a particularly challenging environment when it comes to measuring their digital properties. A digital property might contain a lot of product information, personalization, engaging experiences, design or product ideas, and even social commentary and reviews. We want to know which of those assets actually increased a consumer's likelihood to buy. But if the digital property doesn't have ecommerce, all we can measure is how much content gets consumed, not what impact or lift that content generated. Unlike the omnichannel retailer, who can at least hope to integrate the store and digital experience into a single customer view, the manufacturer who is selling through a channel often has no idea who the end customer is and has no hope of ever owning that data. Getting an end-to-end view of the customer can seem like an impossible dream to a channel seller; fortunately, with proper use of VoC, it's achievable.

Pharma Company Marketing a Drug to Potential Patients

Like other manufacturers, pharmaceutical companies don't sell directly to the consumer. However, when specialty or prescription products are involved, they don't sell to the consumer at all. The consumer *can't* buy the product. For a consumer-focused digital property, that means figuring out how to measure success when the target audience doesn't convert online and might not be able to get the product at all. For these companies, success is often twice removed. The potential patients consuming the content can only get the product if someone else (the physician) also chooses it. These digital properties aren't meant to generate leads—they are meant to start or support conversations with a third party. You can imagine how difficult it is to measure this form of second-hand success.

The idea behind such a laundry list is to emphasize how common it is for the measurement of digital success to depend on understanding what happened outside the digital world. This isn't an edge case: It's much easier to understand what someone was trying to accomplish in the digital world (the visit type or use case) than to figure out whether that user was successful. We can usually recover the visit type and use case from careful analysis of digital behavior; we often cannot measure success without recourse to data outside the digital realm.

Not surprisingly, we have countless ways to support the integration of offline and digital data. Depending on the business and business model, approaches such as registration, email cookies, credit card matching, and loyalty programs can provide data linkages that integrate digital and nondigital data about customers.

Where direct linkages exist, be sure to use them. You might face plenty of challenges, but there is little additional theoretical interest from a measurement perspective. For example, if you can integrate CRM data with digital data, you likely can measure the outcomes of any given lead generation use case. The same goes for any of these use cases where direct behavioral ties between the offline and online world are possible.

Many times those direct linkages don't exist and aren't possible. That's where VoC comes in. With targeted use of online surveys, you can piece together significant parts of the customer journey. Obviously, VoC data isn't like behavioral data; it doesn't exist for every digital visitor and customer. Still, VoC data provides a way to stitch together the journey for enough customers to map the relationship between digital behaviors and downstream success—and that's what really matters.

Sampling and Bias

Before diving further into the use of VoC to measure customer journey, a brief detour into the realm of survey sampling and bias is necessary. Getting a reasonably representative sample is a critical component of survey research. Without a representative sample, you can't extrapolate the results from the research population to the broad population with any confidence. And because VoC research almost always targets a tiny percentage of users, extrapolation is the whole point.

The most common tactic for site surveys is to focus on a subset of visitors who have at least a moderate amount of behavior on the website. That's neither foolish nor surprising: The original intent of most site surveys was to understand the site experience. When companies first discovered the potential for online research, several factors drove them to focus on site experience. First, site experience needed help. As with everything else, web design principles took time to mature and standardize. Until they (sort of) did, there was tremendous demand for feedback on what type of site design and experience worked. Second, asking site visitors other questions about the business or products did little good because digital visitors tended to be extremely different than the general set of customers.

Both of these factors have evolved significantly. It's still important to understand site experience, but these days, digital properties are more standardized, more professional, and more polished. So research around customers in the online space is more likely to focus on understanding their digital needs and how to meet them than trying to figure out where the navigation bar should be. A measurement foundation based on two-tiered segmentation is designed for exactly this kind of customer-focused research, but it should also be clear that VoC is well suited to that research as well. However, this type of research doesn't necessarily require that the user experience much of the site. It's just as valid to explore these questions with visitors who do little on the site or have never even visited it. After all, these days, nearly everyone is a digital user.

So it doesn't necessarily make sense to limit your site surveys by only sampling visitors with a significant amount of onsite behavior.

This brings up the second point. Even as getting a good sample in the nondigital world using traditional techniques such as random-digit dialing and mall intercepts has gotten geometrically harder, the participants in the digital world have become far more representative. With the overwhelming majority of people (at least, here in the United States) digitally experienced and enabled, the gap between the digital and nondigital populations of most businesses has shrunk to something relatively insignificant. That isn't the case everywhere (digital properties that focus on the very old or very poor might still see sharp differences), but it's true most places. So digital surveys can be representative and work to research a much wider range of business issues than the site itself. In the early days of digital surveys, almost the only set of questions that could be reasonably extrapolated from an online survey to the business were questions about the site from site users. That's not true anymore.

Given the challenges of offline sampling, it's a little surprising, and at least partially historical, that online surveys are often considered highly suspect compared to traditional surveys when it comes to representative sampling. Still, concerns about sampling are real and need to be carefully thought through. Online sampling involves biases that you need to understand before you can effectively use online survey research. Indeed, some of the biases are created or exacerbated by the strategies that surround the survey. Others are inherent to the online enterprise—we can never entirely eliminate them, but we can understand and control them.

Two common methods work for making the "ask" for an online survey to potential respondents. The first method is to "ask on entry" and then "pop on exit." You ask respondents whether they'll take a survey when they leave. If they opt in, the survey pops up when they leave the digital property. The second method is to pop the ask or the survey when certain behaviors or triggers are met (such as viewing a certain number of pages).

Both these methods introduce sampling biases. In the second case, the sampling bias is to eliminate all the visitors who didn't meet the minimum consumption threshold. To understand the site experience, that might not be a bad thing. Even with site experience, however, a use case often generates behavior below the ask threshold or does so differentially to other use cases, which creates significant bias. To understand broader product and business questions, this is clearly a significant bias. It's also a bias that's hard to correct for by over-weighting some part of the sample.

With the first method (ask on entry, pop on exit), the bias is considerably more subtle. Because visitors have no experience of the site on the ask, it's possible to introduce a task bias in which visitors in use cases that have a better idea of the business are more likely to accept.

Both methods also have a secondary bias against campaign respondents. Traditionally, visitors who respond to digital campaigns are more likely to abandon a digital property and less likely to be willing to provide feedback. Some enterprises avoid this issue by landing visitors sourced by digital marketing on special landing pages and not making the survey ask there. For a variety of reasons, this strategy just makes things worse.

Also regardless of method, and in all cases of online surveys (and surveys in general these days), there's a broad issue of oversampling engaged populations. In almost all cases, online surveys tend to oversample engaged visitors, or visitors more likely to be strongly positive or strongly negative about their experiences. Integrating survey responses with behavior enables you to observe this effect and measure it. Comparing the amount of behavior and the success percentages by use case for survey respondents to the site average provides a good measure of just how representative the sample is when it comes to the digital population.

Integrating behavioral data with survey data also offers a nice bonus: It provides a good mechanism for oversampling and reducing engagement bias. Overweighting lower behavior respondents can produce a more representative sample of the digital population and control for at least some degree of engagement bias.

With the explosion in market research, there's also a very real phenomenon called survey fatigue. People are tired of taking surveys, and getting adequate response rates can be difficult. Some key techniques for fighting survey fatigue include keeping surveys short, devising more interesting surveys, and offering incentives (when the target population can be controlled by factors such as known customer, known support user, and known blogger).

Of course, any survey ask on your digital properties involves a huge sampling bias that can go almost unnoticed. People on your site are aware of your brand and your products or services and have at least some engagement with your organization. You have no way to run a brand-tracking survey on your website, since 100% of your visitors have heard of you!

If your goal is to research consumer interest in some new product, doing that research on your site biases the sample significantly. I encountered an interesting case of this while doing research for a laptop maker on why customers were shifting to iPads. Online surveys on the site were able to isolate folks who were considering both laptops and iPads, but they inherently missed out on people who'd already decided they no longer needed a laptop. We had to go elsewhere to try to understand that population.

Depending on your research question, the inherent bias of a survey ask on your digital property can be catastrophic (as in brand awareness), damaging (as in the laptop case), or almost completely unimportant (as when researching a customer support question).

No matter what your research question is, it's always critical to think about how representative a sample you can get from an ask and then try to measure how representative a sample you actually do get. For the first, good common sense and a willingness to think about the problems is your best defense. For the second, integrating behavioral data can be a godsend when it comes to measuring and controlling for engagement biases.

Ask Before, Ask During, Ask After

The mantra I use to describe a good VoC strategy is simple: Ask before, ask during, ask after. The basic idea is straightforward. Using

VoC, it's possible to understand where in their journey visitors are when they arrive at a site, where they are when they leave it, and what actions transpire later in their journey. In other words, we can extend our measurement framework beyond the digital world—in particular, to bring measures of success from the outside world into the realm of digital measurement.

Let's start with the first part of the journey: what happens before a visitor arrives at a digital property.

Measuring the Upstream Journey

Site success is down. Conversion rates are down. But the site hasn't changed. The digital marketing hasn't changed. Traffic hasn't changed. What's happening?

This is a question that turns out to be devilishly difficult to answer. A careful study of site behavior will likely yield some partial answers. Perhaps the key shopping use cases are a smaller percentage of site traffic. Perhaps the site has seen a shift from late-stage to early-stage shoppers. A two-tiered segmentation might reveal shifts in the distribution of visitors by either visitor or visit type, and it's a good bet that those changes are impacting the overall success metrics.

This doesn't always work, though. Even when it does, it begs the question of why that shift in distribution is taking place. Here's a situation in which breaking from common practice and targeting short, specific prequalification surveys can dramatically improve digital measurement.

A prequalification survey is typically no more than two to four questions designed to measure and trend the level of interest, knowledge, and commitment of visitors. It's often popped up with no preliminary ask, usually for a relatively small sample. A small sample typically works because the point of the survey isn't behavioral research; it's designed only to provide a trend of visitor qualification levels. The short survey length is critical, to avoid severe undercounting of campaign traffic—especially because marketing-driven traffic is most likely to vary in quality. Ideally, filling out the survey should be almost as easy as killing it.

What is a prequalification question?

This varies by business, but typical qualification questions focus on issues such as the expected time until purchase, brand favorability, and knowledge of specific product(s).

By combining two or three qualification questions, a short survey can create a fairly interesting profile of the visitors entering a digital property. Trending this data over time provides a sharp lens on whether the quality of traffic (in terms of likelihood to succeed in any given use case) is varying. This then illuminates whether site performance is changing for internal or external reasons.

Prequalification measurement is certainly useful for the specific purpose of understanding digital performance. That's not all it can do, however. At one time, people expected a sharp decline in ad spend on traditional (linear) media as everything went digital. That really hasn't happened. Certainly, digital marketing spend has grown steadily—and, in some cases, even quite spectacularly. But most companies that have tried to dramatically scale back traditional media spend (particularly in TV) have seen significant declines in overall media performance and returned to more balanced programs.

As so often happens in the real world, it's more a case of the distinction between linear and digital blurring to the point of indistinguishability. An advertiser buying a program spot these days is typically buying that spot on a mix of platforms that include linear and digital—and, of course, the increasing sophistication of set-top boxes is further blurring the lines.

Nevertheless, a significant amount of media spend is going into places where no individual tracking takes place, and that isn't likely to change for at least a few years. For some companies, a big part of that spend is about driving traffic to digital properties—to investigate, learn, shop, and convert. If that's the case, then measuring prequalification provides an important lens on the performance of those mass media efforts. Mass media isn't the only thing that can change prequalification, but it is the most common variable.

Changes in the macroeconomic climate drive important changes in consumer willingness to buy, especially for certain classes of luxury or big-ticket items. Changes in specific marketplaces (such as housing) can rapidly shift prequalification levels for a related digital property. (I remember doing search engine marketing for mortgage refinancing back in 2008 and seeing programs go from being markedly effective to nearly useless in a matter of months.) Local conditions—even weather—can significantly impact prequalification levels. These days, particularly in technology, market conditions and product competition can change almost instantly and can dramatically alter prequalification levels. The introduction of the iPad memorably shifted the prequalification levels of laptop buyers.

Understanding exogenous factors such as these is important. Sometimes, of course, you can't do much about them. Trying to sell homes in 2008 was a losing proposition, and all the digital performance tuning in the world was as hopeless as trimming sails in a 200 mph storm. That's part of the point, of course. Strategically, knowing what you can't control is as important as knowing what you can.

Tactically, however, things are different. On a tactical level, you can always change the amount and nature of mass media spend and it's often a powerful lever of business performance. When prequalification isn't shifting for macro reasons, it's mostly driven by mass media. That makes careful trending of prequalification to digital properties a good way to measure and tune mass media: It's quicker, more accurate, more segmented, and less costly than traditional media tracking.

Another advantage of prequalification measurement in the digital world is that you can do it locally. Depending on device and privacy settings, digital properties provide different levels of geographic tracking. The most commonly supported level maps to something like a city or Designated Marketing Area (DMA). Almost every visitor to a web property is tracked at least at this level.

Integrating prequalification survey feedback with the underlying digital measurement data makes this level of geomapping consistently available; you can measure the impact and effectiveness of media mix and campaign changes in local markets. That's powerful, and it's one of the places where, in an increasingly integrated world, precise measurement of the digital world can help drive change elsewhere. Most of this chapter is about bringing measurement from outside the digital world into a digital measurement framework (particularly for measurement of success) to get a better understanding of digital behavior. This flow of information, however, is a two-way street.

Targeting Precision

Obviously, a theme of this book (and this chapter, in particular) is that the measurability of the digital world is not always as comprehensive as it appears to be. Tracking individual content consumption is compelling and powerful, but sometimes it raises questions that we can't answer. VoC is a way to fill in some of those gaps.

One of the most frustrating gaps is the frequent lack of intelligence about why a digital campaign performs well or poorly. In the digital world, we pride ourselves on the ability to measure the performance of a marketing campaign and make decisions based on that knowledge. By investing marketing dollars in higher-performing campaigns and eliminating lower-performing efforts, we can greatly improve overall marketing performance.

That's great, but allocation isn't the only method of optimization. Surely it must be obvious that discarding a campaign because it isn't performing well isn't the only possible solution. Sometimes it must be possible to *improve* a campaign, not throw it away.

From the outside, you'd probably expect that most optimization would involve improvement, not elimination, but that isn't the way digital measurement often works. Measuring campaign success provides a very blunt instrument. It can help make a decision to allocate more to a campaign or to stop investing in it; it can't really help figure out how to improve that campaign.

Sometimes two-tiered segmentation can help drive an improvement conversation. For example, understanding the use-case distribution of a campaign can be surprisingly enlightening. Digital marketing operates under the assumption that every campaign respondent is a potential buyer. Real-world measurement nearly always belies that assumption, sometimes dramatically. I remember a brokerage campaign we measured that sought to acquire new accounts. The single most common action for visitors sourced on that campaign was to log in. More than half the respondents were existing customers.

Measuring use case distribution for campaigns is a way to test whether the campaign is sourcing visitors with the expected intent. When it isn't, the campaign nearly always underperforms.

Prequalification is another way to measure why a campaign isn't performing well. Campaigns consist of three key elements: targeting, creative, and offer. Each element is important in driving success. Back in the old direct marketing days, offer was always the most important factor, targeting next, and creative last. Digital and brand marketers often forget this, but it's still largely true.

Without a rich set of controlled experiments, how do you tell which of these elements is driving (or torpedoing) the performance of any given campaign?

One way is to measure the effectiveness of the campaign for different levels of prequalification and compare that to other campaigns. If a campaign has a very high conversion rate for qualified visitors but a much lower percentage of qualified visitors, it's obvious that improving the targeting will improve the overall performance of the campaign. On the other hand, if a campaign fails to convert quali-fied visitors at a satisfactory level, the creative material is the culprit. Measuring prequalification creates a way to separate out the impact of targeting and creative and provides a path to tuning, not just dis-carding, campaigns.

You can further extend this method by deepening the type of information collected in the upfront VoC, beyond the basic prequali-fication questions. Most campaigns are conceived with a specific audience in mind. In the mass media world, that audience is typically quantified via demographics, and then businesses use those demo-graphics to buy spots on content that matches the target. This essen-tially guarantees a certain degree of targeting precision. Because you are buying the audience based on the same variables you targeted them on, the system is likely to deliver the audience you expected.

The process doesn't work that way in the digital world. For the most part, digital buys provide a higher degree of targeting but a less direct mapping of the targeting used in the buy to the targeting used in developing the creative. This lack of ease in mapping from the audi-ence conceived of to the audience actually purchased can account for huge mistakes in digital targeting—and those mistakes can destroy the performance of campaigns.

Extending or adding a small set of demographic profile questions to a prequalification survey can illuminate these issues. Adding a few core targeting questions to an online survey targeted to marketing respondents provides a measure of targeting precision—the degree to which a digital buy's audience matched initial expectations.

What's more, integrating behavioral data with that targeting data makes it a snap to identify what's driving the performance of a cam-paign. Cross-tabulating success rates for respondents inside and out-side the target audience can easily measure whether the campaign works for the target audience and the extent to which the actual audi-ence matches the target.

This concept of targeting precision is a shift in the nature of campaign optimization. It changes the basic methodology of digital marketing optimization from improvement based solely on allocation to improvement based on tuning underperforming campaign elements.

Offsite Survey

A robust VoC program has one last element for upstream journey tracking in the digital world. Prequalification and targeting precision both work off surveys targeted to visitors arriving at a digital property. Sadly, not all of your target audience will ever arrive at your digital doorstep. You have no way to use your online survey program to gain insight into what happens with potential customers who don't visit you.

That's a huge gap.

Fortunately, you have a simple, and mostly ignored method for filling that gap. The digital world is huge, of course. In our household, whenever a discussion breaks out or a question is raised, it's settled by a quick resort to our phones to look something up. And whether the question is "How many movies has Pixar made and which one are we forgetting?" or "Would it be more expensive to fly to Croatia or Ireland this summer?" the answer is rarely more than a few searches away.

With such a huge ocean of content, almost regardless of the space your digital property occupies, other digital spaces overlap and draw relevant audiences to you and your competitors. If you're Ford Automotive, your website will always draw a sample of visitors significantly biased toward Ford in terms of brand awareness and preference. But a third-party automotive site will draw a relevant sample of potential car buyers without that Ford bias built in. Naturally, that makes these third-party sites with overlapping content natural places for buying advertising to reach that upstream audience. It doesn't have to be advertising that you buy, however. These types of sites are superb for deploying online surveys that target your upstream audience.

Using digital to deploy online surveys off your site is still a small part of most companies' research programs. It shouldn't be. It's the easiest, most cost-effective, and most customizable way to reach an unbiased (and potentially very customized and targeted) audience of upstream consumers with a flexible and powerful research vehicle (the online survey).

Offsite surveys open up a host of research questions that just don't make sense onsite. Brand tracking and awareness are two of the most common types of research programs done offsite. However, so much more is possible. With an unbiased sample of potential customers, you can explore why visitors might select your digital property over a competitor's, what types of marketing messages and functionality are most appealing by segment, and where specific competitors excel or struggle.

Prequalification surveys provide a trended view into the quality of traffic reaching a digital property. That view makes it possible to better assess what's driving the overall performance of the property and why that performance is changing. Prequalification is also a way for digital measurement to lend a hand in measuring the effectiveness and optimal mix of mass media buying. Targeting precision extends this concept by adding a few core targeting questions to the VoC survey, to help understand whether targeting or creative is driving campaign performance. By adding targeting precision to the mix in digital marketing, optimization can evolve beyond allocation decisions into optimization decisions. Finally, the use of offsite surveys opens up deep research windows into the upstream journey. In targeting unbiased audiences outside your digital properties, this type of research can help you understand why customers might choose to visit or avoid your digital properties in the first place.

Taken together, these VoC techniques dramatically expand the visibility of the measurement foundation into what happens *before* a visitor enters a digital property and how you can use that upstream behavior to both understand and maximize digital performance.

Measuring Onsite (During)

The traditional site intercept is designed to measure what happened during a digital visit. As such, there's less to say about this area than about VoC for measuring the up- or down-stream journey. Measuring VoC for what visitors just did is standard practice. However, standard practice can be improved in a couple of places.

The biggest weaknesses in most online survey programs lie in the focus and stability of the survey instrument. For historical reasons already discussed, many online surveys focus heavily on measuring the site experience, or how the digital property works as a tool. A popular survey instrument uses dozens of questions on navigation, images, and content to try to measure the site experience at a deep level.

Some of these questions are interesting. Most aren't. But the deeper problem is that, although measuring the site experience as a tool isn't uninteresting, it's better done behaviorally than with VoC— and it's far from the most interesting use of VoC possible.

For example, you might ask visitors whether they like the imagery on your site and whether they think there's enough of it. How much imagery to add to a site is a fairly interesting concern, so why not ask? The problem is, visitors aren't designers. The amount and quality of the imagery and its impact on them isn't what they came to the site to judge (unless it's an art site). That's a bit like asking a customer who's just eaten a complex French dessert if they thought the sauce had the right amount of vanilla. That's not what they were there to judge. What's more, behavioral measures (for example, whether the visitors would order the dessert again and whether they finished it) are usually more reliable and more consistent than even high-level feedback on whether visitors "liked" it.

Back in the early days of web design, digital properties were often so broken that exploring the "tool" using VoC had a real purpose. These days, it mostly doesn't.

Sure, if it were possible to ask *any* number of questions to *any* number of respondents, some exploration of the digital property as a tool would make perfect sense. That usually isn't the case, though. You have a real and substantial opportunity cost to every question you ask and every survey you launch. To get good response rates and avoid fatigue, survey instruments need to be small, interesting, and relatively infrequent for any given customer. What's more, you can ask only occasionally without impacting the rest of the digital experience.

In practice, that means every time you use a survey on the site as a tool, you lose an opportunity to explore more about visitors; who they are, what they care about, and how they make decisions.

Those are precious opportunities lost.

Think about it this way: If you're deploying a single VoC survey in a grocery store, how many questions are you going to ask about the cart? I'm pretty sure the answer is one or less. Imagine a survey that asked about the size of the cart, the size of the wheels, how well they rolled, whether the flap should go up or down, how easy it was to unstack, and whether the return area was large enough. That survey might produce some interesting findings, but it would be tedious and stupid if it was the only survey you ever ran.

That's the way most site surveys work: They focus on the cart, not the customer.

To create a better site survey, rethink your priorities when it comes to VoC research in the digital world. When placed in a rich measurement foundation, behavioral data can answer many key questions of visit intent and success by visitor type. Behavioral data can't figure out what drives the decisions that underlie the distribution of visit types and the relative success of visitors inside those visit types. Behavioral data can decide what content visitors consume and what impacts their behavior. Understanding how that works is much more difficult with behavioral data.

The best role for VoC in the digital world is to fill in those gaps. Questions designed to do that are the ones worth spending precious real estate on.

No single set of questions is right for any business, but here's a little checklist of different types to consider:

- **Product knowledge questions**—Few factors have a bigger impact on buying decisions than consumer knowledge. But estimating consumer knowledge from content consumption is hard in many digital contexts. At best, broad signals emerge. Exploring what knowledge visitors actually have and how that translates into behavior (content consumed, time spent, products chosen) is huge for optimizing the digital property *and* anything you do offline as well. If your online surveys don't spend some time exploring consumer knowledge and then tying it to behavior, you're missing the boat.

- **Brand value questions**—Brand folks love to talk brand value. And why not? Brand is meaningful. In some contexts, brand can be decisive. But just how valuable is the brand? And how do differences in brand perception translate into differences in content consumption and product choice? Brand folks regularly punt on those critical questions. It's always a good idea to have at least one or two brand-exploration questions.

- **Competitive positioning questions**—Competitive positioning questions go hand in hand with brand questions. Few questions reveal more about a customer's decision-making process than what other alternatives that person is considering. Understanding the competitive set casts a huge amount of light on why the customer selected a particular product and whether he or she purchased it. If you're not exploring what else a visitor is considering when using a digital property, you're missing out. Remember that the defining fact of digital is the remarkably low friction involved in going elsewhere. That makes understanding the competitive set—whether it's for products, content, or entertainment—vitally important.

- **Feature value questions**—So much of this discussion seems to be about marketing that it's easy to forget that success in the digital world (and the world in general) isn't always about marketing. A good product at a good price is far more often a pathway to real success than optimized marketing. Shockingly few companies use online research to explore product options and alternatives. Techniques such as conjoint analysis are ideal for discovering optimal feature bundles and tuning product sets. Online surveys provide a natural forum for open-ended and detailed exploration of what people want.

- **Emotional self-categorization questions**—Some of the most interesting segmentation questions in online research involve getting visitors to self-categorize themselves. Are they looking for the "best deal," the "best performance," or the "coolest-looking product?" Understanding which of those self-descriptions best describes shoppers can help explain much about their reactions to different content and types of content. These questions are fundamental to exploring personalization options and helping the business drive different creative approaches.

- **Core demographic and life stage questions**—Yes, these still matter. Sometimes you just want to know how old your audience is. This is largely how creative folks continue to think about people. And although behavioral and deeper attitudinal research is often neglected, it would be wrong to imply that understanding core demographics isn't still a part of VoC research. What's more, these questions can help tie findings to broader marketing and ad spending efforts in which demographics and life stage are the only targeting mechanisms available.

- **Decision-making style questions**—Consumer researchers have long known that people don't all make decisions in the same way. Different people bring different blends of intuition, emotion, reason, and value to the equation of how they make decisions. Understanding those styles can explicate content behaviors and use case success at a deep level. Are folks with a deep need for information more or less successful in a use case than others? That can be a powerful cue to whether the website has sufficient informational content. Learning to identify different styles of decision makers and then build content to support them is another much neglected part of VoC research.

Stability

When it comes to airplanes and astronauts, it's hard to have too much stability. When it comes to survey instruments, it's awfully easy to go overboard. If most digital survey instruments are too focused on the site as a tool and too little focused on the customer, that vice is hugely exacerbated by the fact that they never change. Many organizations run the exact same survey year in and year out, with hardly a change in question. Some survey vendors even require this sort of stability as a core part of their methodology. It's all a huge waste.

Sure, it's nice to be able to trend a few core online research measurements. Prequalification questions, for example, are specifically designed to be trended over time. Ditto for questions on site experience satisfaction or net promoter score (NPS). These types of measurements are mostly about trending, and they need to be stable to be analyzed over time.

For the vast majority of potential questions in an online research program, however, stability is a curse. After you've analyzed a research question, why keep asking the same thing? The overwhelming majority of survey questions show relatively little movement over time. Fixing the survey instrument in a single form means that information consumers get the same report over and over again. You can imagine how well that works.

When judging the quality of a VoC research program, the single most important factor is how often the research program changes. The healthier the program, the more often new questions, new research directions, and new survey instruments are deployed. In 20 years, I've never encountered a survey program that changed too often. It's not impossible to imagine such a beast, but given its rarity, it's pointless to worry about it.

When to Ask: The Role of Targeted Surveys and Samples

Another aspect of stability is a tendency to think about site surveys as a single monolithic opportunity. Over devotion to one methodology (such as ask on entry, pop on exit) can also lead organizations to think there's only one possible survey to deploy. But even if you're committed to one methodology (and that's a mistake), not every respondent should get the same survey.

One nice way to think about a VoC research program is to distinguish between the role of a primary site survey and a range of smaller, short-lived surveys. The primary survey is designed to collect core trending data and to support a broad range of research questions for exploration in conjunction with behavioral data. The smaller, targeted surveys are designed to tackle specific research problems. For the ongoing survey, the types of questions will probably reflect a diverse set across all the questions described in the earlier checklist. More emphasis will fall on stability and trending, and the data set will be constantly available and integrated with behavioral data. That's all great. But a host of questions will never get answered by even the best survey instruments. Ideally, that single site-wide survey should be supplemented with an endless variety of smaller surveys targeted to particular research questions.

These smaller surveys should be custom fitted to the problem they're tackling. If the research problem is to understand why users fall back to internal search for product discovery, the survey should be popped only for search users and the questions should all target that research question. The shorter they are and the deeper they go, the more likely you can get real answers.

Keep in mind that each location in a digital property represents a distinct sample. That sample might be uniquely valuable for answering specific types of questions. I remember a story one company told about its attempt to figure out why customers abandoned the shopping cart. It tried a pop-up survey on cart abandon but found that visitors were largely unresponsive. Getting folks who were leaving a cart to explain why they were doing so was hard. So the company turned the whole experiment around and popped up a survey for visitors who completed a purchase, asking what might have kept them from buying. That population was much more willing to fill out a survey, but of course, they hadn't abandoned. By flipping the question, however, they were able to get a certain kind of intelligence about possible reasons for abandonment from a population that was unquestionably qualified buyers. Is that the same as targeting visitors who abandon? Clearly not. But it's a creative and interesting way to take advantage of the sample you can get.

Popping up a survey to purchasers is a great idea. That sample population is probably more likely to provide information. It's also an inherently valuable population. Of course, it's not a random sample of anything except purchasers. That limits the types of research you can conduct, but it deepens the value of the research targeted to that population. As a general rule, the more targeted a population is, the less useful is the research for broad questions and the more interesting it is for that particular audience.

Sometimes, you can use variations on the ask to help answer questions about the influence of a digital experience. The impact of digital consumption on behavior is generally measurable—often directly from digitally demonstrated behaviors and sometimes from the integration of offline data. Measuring the impact of digital consumption on brand perception is much harder. You can ask brand awareness and perception questions on exit, but how do you know what impact the site visit had on those responses?

One strategy is to create two surveys that explore brand perception, and then pop up one on entry and one on exit to two randomly selected populations. You hold the survey populations constant for demonstrated site behavior and compare brand perceptions between the two controlled samples. Significant differences between the two could be attributable to the immediate site experience.

In an ideal world, an analyst studying a digital property could construct, deploy, and analyze a survey instrument targeted to a specific research problem within a few days, without additional cost, and as nothing more than a part of a broader behavioral analysis. The technology for this type of deep ad hoc integration of VOC research into behavioral analysis is available and easily deployed. The only thing keeping organizations from using it is, in most cases, a complete lack of understanding about why it's necessary.

Benchmarking and Cross-Site Comparison

This chapter is an extended plea for vastly expanded VoC research that is deeply integrated in behavioral measurement. It's particularly annoying, then, that the single most common use of VoC research in the digital realm is almost completely misguided and useless.

For many enterprises, the entire VoC program is used to measure visitors' site satisfaction or NPS and then compare that score to the competition's.

Nothing is terrible about the immediate measurement. Both site satisfaction and NPS capture something fairly interesting about a visitor's attitudes, and that data is worth understanding.

However, trending that data—and, even more, comparing those measurements to the competition's—often involves a fundamental mistake in interpretation that makes the whole exercise worse than useless.

To understand this, you have to go back to the whole nature of online research in the digital realm. In the offline world, survey research firms have been running brand tracking and comparison surveys for many years. In these surveys, the researcher finds a way to approximate a random sample of consumers, asks that sample which brands they recognize and which they prefer, and explores their comparative impressions of those brands.

This works.

It's research based on a single sample that is carefully screened and created independently of any one company's marketing effort or audience. Given that, the comparisons it generates are likely to be correct.

In the digital world, your online site survey is in no way comparable.

Imagine that Ford, GM, and Honda all deploy a site survey and all ask an identical question about a visitor's propensity to recommend the brand. Is the Ford score comparable to the GM or Honda score? Not by a long shot. Even if every aspect of the survey is constant (from the ask method, to the question itself, to the rest of the survey), the samples for each survey are entirely different. Yes, each sample is the set of visitors to a manufacturer's digital property; in that respect, they are similar. But each company has a completely different mix of visitors, use cases, and marketing. Whenever Ford, GM, or Honda launches a new digital campaign, that campaign changes the nature and mix of the visitors coming to that particular digital property—but not to the other properties. When you change the mix of visitors to a website—particularly when you change the distribution of each use case or the qualification level of visitors—you almost certainly change broad measures such as site satisfaction or NPS. Changes in the value of NPS or site satisfaction are almost never caused by actual changes in either the target population or the site experience; they are nearly always artifacts of changes to the underlying sample.

With online digital research, the sample is always changing in response to changes in digital marketing and site design. This is fundamentally different than in traditional offline survey research, and it makes the simple trending of data extremely problematic.

Worse, when you try to do cross-site comparisons to competitors, no data allows you to control for those changes.

The bottom line is simple: Trying to compare top-level measurements such as NPS or site satisfaction across different sites is stupid. It doesn't work because you have no way to isolate the impact of changes in the sample from other potential factors. If your digital analytics team is providing this kind of information to the enterprise, fire the messenger.

If you've followed the argument well, you probably have figured out that this same objection applies to trending these high-level metrics over time for a single site.

That's right.

If you track site satisfaction or NPS over time for a single site, the changes in the measure are nearly always caused more by changes in the underlying sample driven by marketing programs or exogenous factors than by site changes.

This isn't always true, of course. The numbers in the wake of a major redesign, for example, could represent an actual response to the change (although even that is tricky to evaluate and often time dependent—regular visitors tend to react negatively to all site changes). But for the most part, changes in variables such as NPS on a site-wide basis have almost nothing to do with actual changes in digital performance.

Let the information consumer beware.

Of course, for internal measurement of a digital property, this isn't fatal. The segmentation foundation and prequalification methods are designed to isolate subpopulations against which measuring trends in visitor satisfaction is meaningful. VoC KPIs are no more (or less) immune to the problems and drawbacks of site-wide measurement than any other type of metric.

Most enterprise VoC programs already use online surveys to explore attitudes that shape the immediate visit. Where they fail is in the depth and flexibility of those approaches. Recognizing that every place in a digital property presents an opportunity for a unique sample, you have countless opportunities to broaden and deepen measurement of the digital world with highly customized surveys that explore critical problems in customer decision making, brand awareness, and choice. Understanding the power of VoC also demands understanding the limits—and realizing why certain common uses of online surveys on cross-site comparison and over-time trending can be deeply misleading.

Measuring Downstream Value (Ask After)

It bears repeating: Measuring success is essential to proper optimization. That doesn't mean you can pick just any measure of success. People often don't get this, but the truth is that optimizing to the wrong measure is often worse than not optimizing at all. Consider an example. Back in the early days of search engine marketing, paying an agency to drive traffic to the website was common. Okay, that's still common. Back then, however, success was measured by how many visits were generated per dollar spent. The metric for this in pay-per-click programs is cost-per-click. For a long time, cost-per-click was the single most common metric used to optimize search engine marketing programs.

As it happens, cost-per-click is a terrible metric to use for optimization. The problem with cost-per-click is simple and obvious. Some keywords generate better traffic than others (as do some ads). But cost-per-click entirely ignores the quality of traffic generated. Unfortunately, the digital world usually provides plenty of opportunities to generate traffic, and it mostly obeys a pretty simple rule: Bad traffic is cheaper than good traffic. Agencies that were asked to optimize a program on cost-per-click quite naturally did just that. They found the worst, cheapest traffic they could and spent as much money as possible on it.

Does that sound like a good program?

A few years back, we routinely measured programs in which the immediate abandonment rate for a search click-through was 70, 80, or even 90 percent. The reason for this was pretty consistent: The agency had found a really cheap source of bad traffic.

What's funny about this is that the agency was doing its job. If you're asked to optimize to a metric and that's how your performance is judged, that's what you do. If the metric is a bad one, aggressive optimization will often make a program much worse than if it was simply set up with a good-faith effort to make it reasonable. If the performance of an agency is measured by cost-per-click, it's just unreasonable to complain if the quality of traffic from those clicks stinks. It might seem paradoxical, but in the absence of the right success metrics, data-driven decision making is often much worse than unguided instinct.

It's worth one last plain statement: Getting the right measurements of success is the single most important part of an analytics program.

What does it take to get the right measurement of success? Well, going back to the first part of this chapter, it often requires integrating the downstream measurement of success into the measurement of digital behavior. For everyone from manufacturers, to pharmaceutical companies, to technology sellers, to broadcasters, the success of the digital experience can be completely understood only by measuring subsequent nondigital behavior.

One way to understand downstream success is to measure it at the individual level. That's the big data approach, and in many respects, it's the best possible approach. When you can track every individual from online to offline, you have a perfect view into how online behavior drove to offline success. On the other hand, the big data approach is expensive, time consuming, and, in some cases, flat-out impossible. That's where VoC comes in.

Resurvey Techniques

A survey program typically consists of a multitude of ad hoc small, targeted surveys and a single, more comprehensive survey that is designed to support a variety of research questions. For sites that don't have the built-in ability to track visitors over time (as most logged-in sites do, for example), the one question never to omit from the comprehensive survey is the resurvey question. The resurvey question is simple: It simply asks whether the respondent would be willing to take another survey later. If the answer is yes, it's followed by a request for an email address.

That's it.

This simple question provides a means of connecting downstream behavior to current web sessions. With that connection comes a powerful tool for understanding downstream success and the digital behaviors that predict and perhaps drive it.

The opt-in from a survey request provides an easy mechanism in which you can send a second survey (the resurvey) to the visitor. That survey is typically sent after some significant time period has elapsed—usually long enough for a typical sales cycle to play out. For big-ticket items with long sales cycles, waiting six or eight weeks before sending a resurvey might be best. Smaller-ticket items that require rapid decisions might warrant a resurvey in days or weeks.

That second survey is nothing like the initial site survey. First, because it's linked to the initial site survey and to site behavior, there's no need to re-ask any background questions. Second, the purpose of the resurvey is specifically to track outcomes and the reasons that drove those outcomes.

Typically, that means exploring what site visitors have done since the visit. Did they buy a product? If so, which one? How much did they spend? If they chose a competitor, why? What channel did they use to make the purchase, and who did they buy from? These types of downstream action questions are all about getting at success. It would be foolish not to spend a little effort exploring why those actions came about, but the real key from a digital standpoint is the simple capture of downstream success.

With the resurvey, an analyst now has a clear connection for a sample of visitors, with three critical data points. The first data point is the initial site survey response that provides information on who the visitors were, their qualification level, and their decision-making process. The second data point is the collection of measured digital behaviors—what they did on the digital property. A critical part of this second data point is the organization of that behavioral data into the two-tiered segmentation of our measurement foundation. The final point is the resurvey data about final outcomes and the value of those outcomes.

Combined, these three data points make for a powerful model. By cross-tabulating use case with downstream value, it's easy to calculate the average value of a visitor in each use case. By matching site behaviors to downstream value, you can show which digital behaviors are a good predictor of downstream value. By modeling the impact of site behaviors on downstream value when controlled for prequalification, you can make some assessments on whether digital behaviors are just correlated to success or actual drivers of it.

Each of these three results is huge:

- **Cross-tabulating use case with downstream value**—How valuable is it to source a customer into a specific use case? The answer to that question determines the shape of your digital marketing program. Different display and PPC programs almost always target audiences with a different distribution of use cases. To understand which of those programs to invest in, it's necessary to understand the cost of each program, the type of audience the programs source, and the value of that audience. In one memorable use of resurvey techniques for a home improvement manufacturer, we found that visitors sourced for a set of use cases that involved design and planning functions were more valuable downstream than visitors sourced for use cases of finding a store from which to buy. This contravened years of subjective optimization in which the goal had been to optimize digital marketing programs to source visitors at the "where to buy" stage.

The difference in downstream value wasn't slight. Design users turned out to be far more valuable and involved in far larger purchases than the "where to buy" crowd. So even though any individual respondent was less likely to actually end up making a purchase, the average order sizes more than compensated for the difference.

This fundamentally changed the optimization strategy for the digital marketing program. Knowing how valuable the visitors in each case actually are can drive investment decisions in tools

and content for those use cases, test plan optimization and pri-
oritization, and digital marketing optimization.

• **Identifying which digital behaviors predict downstream
value**—The single most controversial, challenging, and annoying concept in digital measurement is engagement. When
people can't measure downstream outcomes, they still need
some way to measure success. Inevitably, that just means measuring digital content consumption and using it as a proxy for
success. It's usually pretty obvious that measuring page views
or time onsite doesn't work, so this gets called engagement
instead—even when *engagement* just means measuring page
views or time onsite. *Engagement* is a catchall term meant to
suggest measuring some optimal mix of consumption. In some
respects, this search for a proxy makes perfect sense. But use
of the *engagement* word often hides the subjective choice of
a proxy that, if exposed, would be universally viewed as inad-
equate. With resurvey data, it's possible to model which behaviors inside each use case actually predict downstream value.
The full range of potential behavioral proxies (from page type
consumption, to pattern of consumption, to amount of total
consumption) can be explored and correlated to downstream
value. The beauty of this approach is that the proxy for success is no longer subjective. It's chosen based on real evidence
that links it to actual value. Just to be clear, no claim in this
analysis asserts that the digital behaviors cause the value. Correlation is not causation, and that's definitely true in this case.
Fortunately, when searching for a proxy measure of success,
there's no need for causation. Many analysis projects work only
if it turns out that correlation is also causation. That isn't the
case here. In looking for proxy success measures, the goal is
to understand, for example, which digital marketing campaigns
sourced the best visitors. If a digital behavior is strongly correlated to downstream success and one marketing campaign

sourced more visitors who did that behavior, then it's probably a better campaign (cost being equal). It doesn't matter whether the digital behaviors were themselves causal.

- **Modeling the impact of site behaviors on downstream value when controlled for prequalification**—Wouldn't it be nice, though, if we also had a way to understand which digital behaviors did drive downstream value? The previous proxy method is great for optimizing digital campaigns, but it's useless for optimizing the content on the digital property. Suppose it's true that exiting after viewing a single product page is more strongly correlated to downstream value than viewing three or more product pages (a true example from one analysis). That doesn't mean forcing visitors to exit after they first view a product page will increase their value. Controlled experiments in conjunction with resurvey provide a powerful method for answering these causal questions once and for all. Even without controlled experiments, however, we can derive partial answers by incorporating the prequalification concepts into the model. By analyzing which site behaviors are correlated to downstream value when prequalification is held constant, you have some means of actually driving toward causality.

Sampling Challenges

Is it really that easy? For a technique that answers questions at the core of digital measurement, resurvey seems almost too easy. It isn't. The world rarely fails to challenge us, and most methods (including resurvey) turn out to be harder than they look. The actual mechanics of resurvey are simple indeed. The additional ask is trivial; when you've got email addresses, sending out a follow-up survey and combining the three data points should be straightforward. The real challenge in resurvey work involves the sample.

As already discussed, every online sample tends to overweight for engaged customers. Resurvey exacerbates that bias. This impacts some uses of resurvey more than others. For example, when cross-tabulating use case with downstream value, the actual value measurements are almost certain to significantly overestimate the value of a use case visitor. What's more, different use cases could have biases in how likely visitors are to respond to surveys and to accept a resurvey request. On the other hand, when identifying which digital behaviors predict downstream value, it's much less likely (but not impossible) that resurvey biases will impact the analysis. For example, when choosing between whether time on a product page or number of product pages viewed is a better proxy success, one population is not likely significantly different in its propensity to accept a resurvey request.

Digital analysts also have an advantage when it comes to VoC in general: the ability to use behavioral data to evaluate the representative nature of a sample. For example, behavioral data measures the percentage of visitors in each use case that accept both a survey request and a resurvey request. Behavioral data also measures the differential in behavior between respondents and decliners of a survey and a resurvey. Where behavioral data doesn't show significant profile differences between respondents, it's a little easier to accept the representativeness of the resurvey data. It's also possible, using the behavioral data, to oversample resurvey groups to adjust the findings and control for the inherent bias of the method.

This takes work.

It would be a mistake to present, for example, the estimated dollar value of a visitor in a use case based on resurvey data without both warning of the dangers and making a real effort to control for survey bias. However, the possibility of survey bias doesn't cut equally along every use of resurvey. The ability to control the bias and drive meaningful answers to critical questions makes this a key part of any digital measurement program that needs to incorporate offline success.

These three techniques combine to create a model of downstream success tied to digital behavior. They bring downstream behavior into the measurement foundation and provide a previously unseen glimpse into the complete user journey. With them, it's possible to measure the value of each site use case, identify the best proxy measurements for digital success inside a use case, and even identify digital behaviors that might increase the likelihood of downstream success. These are all tremendously important. They make the difference between creating a digital measurement program whose single most important ingredient (choosing the right measure of success) is a subjective, hit-or-miss proposition and creating one whose measures of success are firm, data driven, and deeply tied to real business outcomes. No part of a VoC program is more transformative or useful to a measurement foundation than resurvey.

Ask before, ask during, ask after. That's the mantra for incorporating VoC into a digital measurement program. It's a terrible mistake to believe that behavioral measurement is the only part of exploring the digital world, that big data is all there is. For many measurement cases, the ability to "just ask" turns out to be a huge advantage. It can help analysts build the core behavioral measurement foundation, prove it to the organization, and feel confident that it captures something real. Even better, it can create a view of the customer journey that transforms the digital measurement foundation by adding a picture of what happens up- and down-stream of the digital property to the model. For many types of digital properties, this is absolutely essential to measuring success. And, of course, the proper measurement of success is the single most important ingredient in getting measurement right.

8

Big Data and Measuring the Digital World

You've heard the hype. Big data will solve every problem. It'll transform your organization and create unimaginable profits. How much of what you hear about big data is real, and how much is just hype? For that matter, just what is big data, and where does it fit into digital measurement and the framework described here? Analysis of digital behavior turns out to be a paradigm case of big data. In this chapter, we look at why that is—what people (should) mean when they talk about big data and what that means about big data in general.

You measure the digital world by understanding how the behavior recorded in the world translates into understanding who people are and what they are trying to accomplish. This framework isn't technology dependent. It was developed and refined over many years, analyzing many types of digital property with many types of tools. In one sense, the choice of your technology, from Hadoop to Google Analytics, matters no more to the approach than does the selection of a rule or tape measure to measure length. One tool might be more convenient or more powerful than another, but the goal of the measurement is unchanged.

The period between 2013 and 2015 saw tremendous growth in interest in analytics and a great deal of discussion on the power of big data. As with any discussion that leaps the boundaries of technical conversation into the realm of websites, newspapers, and even broadcast media, much that is said is worthless. When companies have a "big data" technology to sell or a "big data" service to provide, there is little interest or reason for precision in what big data is and whether it actually matters.

It is neither fair nor reasonable, however, to judge an argument by its worst proponents. Just because hype and marketing excess swirl around the notion and concept of big data like snowflakes in a blizzard doesn't mean the concept itself is flawed or empty.

During the rise of big data as a concept, the world of digital analytics has seen two huge changes. First, many enterprises began to demand direct access to digital data at the lowest levels. By taking a data feed from an existing digital analytics solution, an enterprise can obtain detailed information about every single digital measurement taken (typically, every page viewed, and sometimes even finer-grained detail than that). Two factors drive most of this interest in getting access to the detailed digital data. First, direct access to the data opens up deeper statistical methods of analysis and the opportunity to build data-driven segmentations to support a two-tiered segmentation framework. Most software-as-a-service digital analytics solutions provide rich reporting, but the analytic and segmentation capabilities can be limited, and it's not always possible to get at the data in the manner analysts prefer. The second factor driving this move toward direct data access is the desire to integrate digital data into broader views of the customer. Where significant nondigital data about the customer resides in internal systems, it's often easier to combine digital and nondigital data outside the digital analytics solution.

The second huge change in the digital analytics world is really driven by the first. Companies have increasingly adopted Hadoop-based systems on which to park that detailed digital data. The move toward open-source, massively parallel data systems and away from traditional relational architectures has happened in lock-step with the demand for digital data.

Is parking digital data on Hadoop big data? And if it is big data, does it matter?

If there were a sound, agreed-upon definition of big data, this would likely be a pretty easy question to answer. There isn't. The phrase *big data* is used carelessly and can mean almost anything in common dialogue. A fairly common working definition, known as the Four V's, is both subjective and flawed in conception. The idea behind the Four V's is that big data is defined by a set of factors—volume, velocity, variety, and veracity—that work separately and in tandem to drive traditional IT and analytics problems into a new space. Some of these factors are almost self-explanatory. Volume, for example, is just the amount of data you have. If you have a lot, you're in big data territory. The definition of "a lot" is fairly subjective. Velocity refers to the speed at which data accumulates. The closer you get to real time and the more data is coming in on a constant basis, the higher the velocity. Variety is designed to capture the complexity of integrating multiple data sources. The more different kinds of data you have (especially data in fundamentally different formats or data that is largely unstructured), the more variety you have. Veracity is meant to describe the accuracy of the data and the challenges involved in handling data with relatively low quality. None of these dimensions has an explicit "big data" threshold, nor must every dimension be significantly exercised for a problem to be widely agreed upon as big data.

The concept of the Four V's is pretty obviously a squishy, unsatisfactory kind of definition. Even worse than its squishiness, though, is that it doesn't really capture anything interesting. The problems of volume, variety, velocity, and veracity have been with us since the dawn of IT. No doubt, we deal with more volume now than ever, and that volume has grown geometrically. Still, the systems we use to process that data have grown geometrically in power and sophistication, and the costs per processing unit and storage unit have shrunk dramatically. Does one trend offset the other? It's hard to know, but there's really no reason to accept that the relationship between the volume of data and the cost of processing power has shifted in some fundamentally negative fashion that makes life measurably worse or more difficult.

Similar observations can be made for variety and velocity. Variety certainly creates IT challenges. It always has and probably always will. What's unclear is whether most big data problems are driven by a new and dramatic increase in the variety of data sources or whether those challenges have morphed in the past decade into something fundamentally new. The same is true for velocity. Achieving real-time speed is indeed hard. But many systems that are widely described as big data systems have no particular velocity challenges, and systems that need to provide a lot of real-time processing are often fundamentally different than those that don't in architecture and intent. It feels more like real-time systems are a distinct problem set that crosses over or perhaps transcends big data. Veracity is likely the weakest member of the quartet (and isn't always included, reducing big data to a mere trio of subjective players). Inaccurate data is certainly the bane of analytics in general, but poor data quality is to analytics what venereal disease is to sex. It has always been with us, will likely always be with us, and has occasioned grief to every generation of participant. To suggest that poor data quality is unique, especially endemic, or even particularly special in big data problems seems unlikely.

In other words, if the Four V's are all there is to big data, it looks a lot like big data is just a bunch of traditional IT problems that vendors have repackaged for marketing purposes into something generational.

Here's another way to think about the question. The digital world generates huge volumes of data. After wearables and machine sensor data, measurement of the digital world (the web—fixed, mobile, and social) probably generates the most data per user of any application and likely generates more total data than any other application. So we have volume. Digital has tremendous velocity. An active digital property generates a flood of data, night and day, in a nearly constant stream. So we have velocity. Nor does the digital world lack variety. With the various digital delivery platforms, the never-ending variety of social media channels (each with its own distinct data), and the plethora of additional sources from content management systems, search engines, and digital marketing systems, there are enough different digital sources to keep an IT team busy with data integration and transformation tasks pretty much forever. So we have variety. To cap it all off, few analytics areas have as many data quality issues as digital. Not to brag, but the poor quality of digital data is legendary. So we have veracity (lack thereof).

By standard definition, then, measuring the digital world ought to be a paradigm case of big data. So it's interesting to ask whether anything in digital measurement is really different, challenges traditional IT or analytics paradigms, and can be associated with (at least some of) the Four V's in a way that would make clever people confuse the Four V's with something more interesting and fundamental (i.e., an error theory).

If the way to measure the digital world is the type of framework described here, then if big data is anything real, aspects of creating this framework should deeply challenge traditional aspects of IT, analytics, or both.

As it happens, they do.

What's Really Different about Analyzing Digital Data

With most traditional analysis, at the heart of the data is a record like Figure 8.1.

Figure 8.1 Traditional data structures

I've chosen a customer record for illustration. Each row represents a single customer and has a set (sometimes a very large set) of columns (fields) associated with it. What's important isn't that this is a customer record—it could be a record for a salesperson, a region, a product, or even a time period. What's important is that each row captures the fundamental unit of meaning in the analysis and that the rows themselves are independent. This is by far the most common situation when it comes to analytics. Indeed, most analytic techniques require that the data be in this type of format.

Digital data doesn't work this way. It doesn't really work this way at a micro level (at the page view or event level), and it particularly doesn't work this way when it comes to the creation of a broader digital journey. With digital data, the meaning is often implicit in the way the data is sequenced (see Figure 8.2).

In the first data set, a visitor navigates through the category page to a product page but then searches for the category page and exits. This looks like a failed session, with the visitor not finding what he or she needed. On the second visit, the user starts with the search and then goes to the category and product pages before exiting. Here, it looks like the user might have found what he or she was looking for. Interestingly, if you just stored the pages a visitor accessed, the two sets of data would look identical. The exact same pages are viewed in each visit. Only the order is different. With most traditional data structures, the order in which things happened isn't represented. For example, our original customer record has no ordering information in the fields. Each field is attached to the customer equally, with no indication which came first.

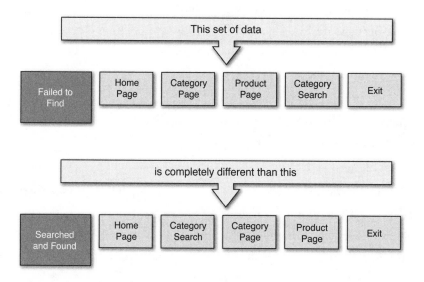

Figure 8.2 When the sequence of data matters

Figure 8.3 shows another example that focuses on the broader user journey.

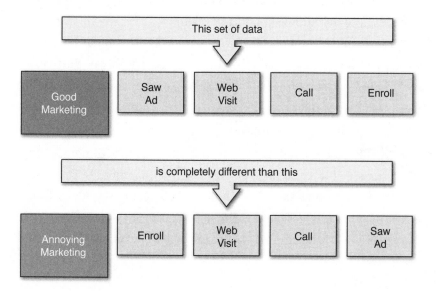

Figure 8.3 Customer journeys are all about sequence

You know this feeling, right? Someone is calling to sell you some-thing *after* you've already purchased it! That's not good.

But the touches themselves are identical in these two sequences, and if all we stored was a set of flags to indicate which events a user had, there would be no way to distinguish between fundamentally different situations.

This isn't terribly puzzling. From a database perspective, it's easy to handle this situation: Just create one row for each event with a date/time stamp to capture the sequence.

Problem solved.

But the problem isn't solved from an analytics perspective, because the meaning of the journey no longer resides in a discrete row. Now the analytics technique needs to be able to combine one or more rows to understand what's happening with the sequence. That's just not the way most analysis techniques work.

You might be thinking that this feels like a time-series analysis, but it isn't really a traditional time-series analysis at all. Yes, time is now a part of the data set, but it doesn't work quite the way most time-series analysis works. Our situation doesn't reflect equal units of time (such as weeks), and although not all time-series methods require that, it's the most common situation. Nor is our situation univariate, as with prices for a stock or sales by day. The vast majority of time-series techniques focus on univariate data. Worse, our multivariate data isn't measured over similar pieces of time, so even most multivariate time-series techniques aren't appropriate.

In other words, digital data introduces a sequence dimension that most statistical analysis methods can't easily capture. It isn't quite like time-series analysis. What's more, introducing sequence forces a relational data structure that prevents aggregation to a single row. That makes many traditional relational database tasks both harder and much less efficient.

Overall, sequence matters in digital data. Sequence is a challenge to traditional data structures and most analysis techniques.

Adding sequence isn't the only challenge in analyzing digital data. Figure 8.4 illustrates another example that's similar, but with one new twist.

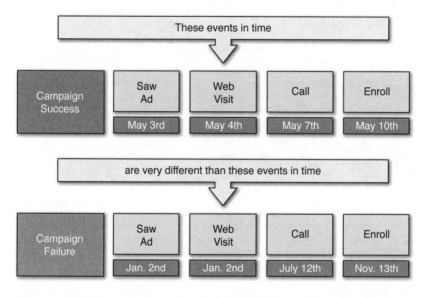

Figure 8.4 When the time between events matters

In this scenario, the events and their sequence are identical, but the time between the events has materially altered the interpretation. If a visitor converted 11 months after a campaign, there's precious little chance the campaign had much influence on that person.

From a database perspective, this doesn't really matter much. After all, once the table structure has become row based with a date/time stamp, the time between is preserved and readily available. On the analytics front, however, it's a considerable new complexity.

When both time between and sequence are in play, it's difficult to compare and analyze any two sets of behavior and make even simple determinations about whether they are the same, or how similar they are. With time between and sequence both considered, few digital journeys of any length are identical. This puts a premium on understanding which journeys are similar in terms of content by sequence and time between. It's hard.

And it gets harder. Often analysis of digital behavior assigns significance to a pattern of events, and that pattern is not just a matter of ordering. Consider Figure 8.5.

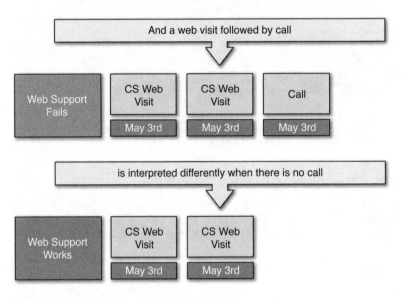

Figure 8.5 When the pattern of events matters

In this example, the presence or absence of a call after a web visit determines whether the web visit is considered successful. That might seem fairly simple, but Figure 8.6 illustrates a more complicated pattern.

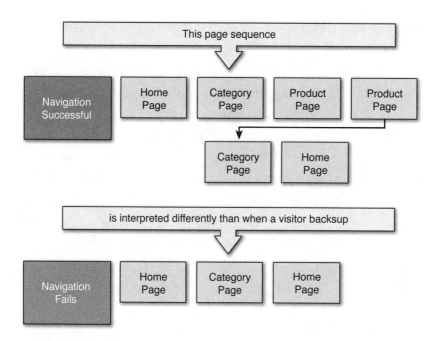

Figure 8.6 When the pattern of events matters (and the pattern is complicated)

In this example, the bounce back from category page to home page generally indicates an unsuccessful navigation path, with the potential interpretation that the user was mistaken in choosing that path. But in the first instance, the drill-down from category page to product page confirms the intent of the original navigation. So even though the user eventually moves back to the category page and then the home page, the visit intent is likely to be driven by the consumption of the category page. Both sequences contain home page, to category page, to home page, but the remainder of the pattern changes the interpretation.

Pattern is kind of a superset of sequence and time between. It encompasses them and extends them. I prefer to think of each separately only because many problems in digital interpretation are heavily focused on sequence and time between. At the broadest level, though, it's fair to say that pattern identification and matching is fundamental to digital analytics.

I chose these examples to reflect two levels common in digital measurement. Getting a good understanding of what happened in a digital visit (the use case) often involves pattern matching to understand what the sequence of page touches means. In that exercise, order, time between, and the pattern of content consumed all might be critical in revealing intent or determining success. This is really the lowest level of digital measurement.

One level up, however, the exercise repeats. To understand a visitor over time, a sequence of touches becomes critical. Presumably, the *who* dimension doesn't change, but the intent dimension now becomes an array of points for every single visitor (see Figure 8.7).

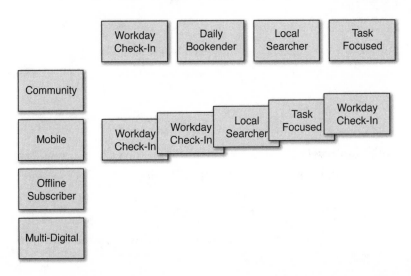

Figure 8.7 Mapping a customer journey as a sequence of visits

A single visitor classified as a mobile user might have a series of digital touches, each classified in a two-tiered segmentation by its intent. What's cool is that these touches, in turn, form a journey much like the sequence of page events that were analyzed to form the original use case classification for each visit. It's a journey in which the order, time between, and pattern of events are important.

This shouldn't be surprising. Viewing a bunch of pages on a web visit is, in fact, a kind of journey. Having a sequence of digital and nondigital interactions with a single enterprise in the digital world is a kind of journey, too.

The same methods of analysis, problems of data structure, and type of pattern-matching techniques apply to measuring and understanding what happens inside and across a visit. The structure of the problem is the same. In both cases, the key is that meaning resides in the relationship between the individual data points, not at the level of the data points themselves.

Introducing sequence, time between, and pattern into an analytics problem changes it. It changes the way data structures have to be laid out. Aggregation with traditional means becomes too lossy because preserving sequence, time, and pattern is almost impossible. This puts a premium on an analytics platform that can retain data at the most detailed level and pass or analyze it rapidly.

At the same time, the unit of meaning no longer lives at the row level; it resides in the relationship (sequence, time, pattern) between the rows. That means a whole bunch of traditional statistical analysis methods aren't applicable out of the box. You can't use regression, correlation, decision trees, or even clustering.

If something at the foundation of digital measurement creates deep challenges to both traditional data processing methods and traditional analytics methods, it seems like a good candidate to be "big data." The existence of sequence, time, and pattern as fundamental to the interpretation of digital data does create just that sort of challenge.

How good of a candidate is it?

Big Data Use Cases

Digital might be a paradigm case of big data, but it's not the only one. If the key to big data is driving data down to a level at which the unit of meaning resides in the pattern between events, that ought to show up in other commonly accepted "big data" problems.

In at least a couple other core big data problems, it does.

One of the biggest problems of big data analytics is machine sensor data. Most complex machines these days include sensors that track their key functioning. Whether it's airplanes, automobiles, gas lines, electricity meters, robots, or locomotives, it's a good bet that somewhere inside, an array of sensors is spinning out data on the internal state of the machine or your consumption. Sensors spin out a gargantuan amount of information and typically have high velocity. On the other hand, variety and veracity aren't major issues when it comes to analyzing this data.

What is a huge issue, however, is that sensor data, as with digital data, drives the level of meaning down into the relationship between the lowest levels of the data. A single sensor reading might have importance as an alert if it goes out of bounds, but from an analytics perspective, all the intelligence lies in the pattern of sensor readings. In a smart meter, for example, it's pretty much useless to know what fraction of a kilowatt-hour a customer used in the last 15 minutes. It's possible to aggregate smart meter data (unlike digital data), but that isn't too intriguing, either. Just adding up the usage to a monthly or quarterly level doesn't take advantage of the detailed 15-minute collection; it just yields the same total usage number per customer that dumb meters have always provided. Sure, it saves money on the meter reading, but analytically, that doesn't matter. The intelligence in this data lies in the way the patterns of usage track to time of day and to season, and how the patterns evolve over time. It lies in patterns and the relationship between readings over time.

That's not at all different in the next big literal thing: the Internet of Things (IoT). The IoT is just sensor data moved broadly into the consumer world, whether via wearables or smart refrigerators. As such, it's just like big machine sensor data—the data has almost identical challenges, and the analytics are all about patterns.

Suppose you need to interpret movement data for a fitness app taken off a smartphone. The underlying data is a rich stream of detailed measurements of time, location, and perhaps heart rate. No single reading is meaningful or particularly interesting. What's key is the relationship between the readings.

Because this health data is understandable in a way that digital data sometimes isn't, it's worth pointing out another aspect of the analytics here. Before it's possible to understand anything about the user, it's necessary to understand what specific patterns in the data mean. One pattern is indicative of running, another of walking, another of riding an elevator, another of circling a kitchen while cooking. People engage in countless activities, and many require significant data interpretation to identify and classify appropriately. Only when those activities have been classified is it possible to say anything interesting about the overall fitness and activity of the user.

This is analogous to the role of two-tiered segmentation in digital data. The use case segmentation is, in effect, analyzing specific patterns of behavior to assign them a purpose. That's the pattern identification step. By stringing those visits together, it's possible to say something about the visitor.

Whether it's the Internet of Things, industrial sensor data, or digital analytics, the data presents a similar and very new challenge. In each and every case of what we commonly think of as big data, traditional analytic techniques have been largely replaced by pattern identification. We can't store any of these data streams in relational structures, and we can't aggregate them without losing the critical meaning captured in the pattern of the events themselves.

It seems, then, that the paradigm cases of big data share a deep similarity in the analytic and IT challenge they present. Whether it's digital, industrial sensors, or the IoT, the data that these systems generate drives the level of analysis down into a very granular level where meaning resides only in the pattern of events.

How does this relate to the Four V's?

Why Everyone Gets It Wrong

That's where error theory comes in. Whether sensor or digital, it's not hard to see why volume is nearly always associated with these problems. It's not that the collection of detailed event data *must* generate a lot of volume—after all, some websites don't attract many visitors. Analyzing their data presents the same analytic challenges as analyzing data from a top 10 web property. It's just that the collection of detailed event-level data is highly likely to present volume challenges. When you go from reading a meter once a month to reading it 3,000 times a month, you've necessarily expanded your data set by several orders of magnitude—hence the confusion surrounding big data and the belief that volume is the problem. Volume is a problem, but it's not the hard or interesting one.

The story around velocity is almost identical. Each of these cases just happens to generate streams of real-time data. For many years, digital analytics solutions competed on their ability to measure that stream of digital data in real time. It was hard, and it limited the ability of those systems to actually filter and analyze the data. After a while, most solutions gave up and most users stopped caring. The fundamental fact about digital analytics, it turned out, wasn't velocity. There *was* plenty of velocity, but for the most part, nobody cared whether the data was loaded in real time or was saved up and batch-processed in the manner of data at rest. Given the nature of the data generated in digital and sensors, it's not hard to see how velocity got tangled up with the idea of big data.

Variety is a different sort of beast. Digital does generate real problems with the variety of sources. That's been particularly true in the last few years, with the explosion of social media alternatives. Still, many enterprises focus on a single digital analytics platform that generates a single data stream—and that's true in most sensor-based analytics applications, whether industrial or IoT based. On the other hand, analysts have generally recognized the importance of external data to provide context for these data streams. As Chapter 4, "Customer Identity and Taxonomy," makes clear, it's almost impossible to intelligently understand stream data without additional context data. That context data often creates integration challenges for IT shops and could be part of the reason variety is considered a common artifact of big data. The nature of detailed stream data also challenges traditional database join strategies. Common equijoin strategies don't work well with stream data, especially if the goal is to join two different streams (such as web and mobile data). If joins are a challenge, variety becomes a real IT burden because the single biggest challenge with multiple data sources is nearly always how you put them together.

Of the Four V's, veracity is the trickiest to rationalize with error theory. If the essence of big data is a new analytics challenge created by a certain kind of detailed data, it's hard to explain why veracity emerges as a particular challenge. That's especially true because nearly all big data is machine generated and is often much more consistent than data sources with more human influences. Not that machine-generated data is immune to data quality challenges—far from it. If digital is indeed a paradigm case of big data, it certainly has its share of data quality issues. Those issues are mostly an artifact of the collection infrastructure and the challenges of the open web (where, for example, robotic traffic is artificially incented by marketing programs), not problems with machines failing to produce consistent data. If there's a clean data source in this world, though, I've never found it. The best error theory I have for why some people think veracity is a unique aspect of big data is that data quality is to blame for at least half our challenges in any kind of measurement and analytics—and that *veracity* happens to begin with a V.

Getting by with What You Have

Every measurement tool is different. In the digital world, measurement tools change with startling rapidity. Regardless of the tool, though, its best possible use depends on understanding how digital measurement works. You must understand how it's possible to interpret digital actions into an understanding of the people doing them, and their intentions. You also must understand how to measure success and then adapt the digital experience to the needs of your users and your business.

Chapter 3, "Use Cases and Visit Intent," logically described the method of mapping behaviors to use cases as a kind of rule-building exercise. That's the best way to understand how measurement works. It also maps fairly well to the method of filtering and segmentation that the most common digital analytics tools support.

Implicit in that discussion was the notion that factors such as sequence, time, and pattern matter. We didn't really address the degree to which we can analyze those elements and the methods by which they are statistically derived.

Most filtering methods can identify and use only basic patterns in the data. As we saw in Chapter 6, "Attitudes and Behaviors: Mixing a More Powerful Measurement Cocktail," it's possible to use VoC data—specifically, a visitor's stated visit intent—as the target variable for a behavioral model. Having a target variable for visit intent makes supervised learning methods (like logistic regression) practical. Clustering provides an alternative approach (unsupervised) that identifies sets of behaviors that tend to group together and that we can then interpret as a use case. Although these methods are quasi machine learning, they are also standard analysis methods in almost any stats package; well-trained analysts widely use and understand them. However, these methods don't do a great job at preserving or analyzing the types of sequence, time, and pattern relationships that frequently matter a great deal in the digital world at both the intrasession and intersession levels.

Techniques for integrating sequence, time, and pattern are presently very unformed and at the bloodiest edge of digital analytics practice. Techniques for sequence labeling (from speech recognition) could be appropriate. Markov and Bayesian models and a priori and deep learning methods are the types of techniques that seem potentially interesting. Image-matching techniques could be useful. The state of the art is too little advanced to know for sure.

Using advanced statistical methods and machine learning techniques sounds pretty cool, but methods are no substitute for understanding. To use any of these methods well, to understand when and why they might be appropriate, and to take real advantage of what they offer, you first must understand the problem and the general nature of the solution.

These advanced analytic techniques are potentially useful precisely because they offer ways to model sequence, time, and complicated patterns in a more natural fashion. I don't think using these methods will replace or much alter the measurement foundation described here—they'll just make them easier to build and more accurate.

Necessity is truly the mother of invention. A good analyst with a proper understanding of the methods for measuring the digital world can usually do far more interesting work with a poor tool than someone with little understanding of the problem but the world's most advanced machine learning techniques at his or her fingertips. It's ideal, of course, to have both.

9 —————————————————————

Omnichannel Analytics

We've shown how the concept of two-tiered segmentation is fundamental to effective digital measurement. It underpins reporting and analysis at almost every level. Now we're going to extend that foundation into the omnichannel world by treating each channel as part of a larger, integrated journey with its own segmentation. Every visit type is part of a larger journey stage. By addressing that dimension, we create a three-dimensional segmentation that has a built-in sequencing component. As we've seen, that's critical to effective big data analytics. In this chapter, we bring together the key elements of the measurement framework to create a comprehensive measurement paradigm across digital spaces.

We can sum up the theme of the previous chapter as "digital analytics is hard." It's hard because the type of data captured lives at a very low level (beneath the level of meaning) and is difficult to analyze with many of the analyst's traditional tools. The two-tiered segmentation approach is designed to meet that challenge and provide a way to effectively measure the digital world. To this point, however, the segmentation has focused on how to understand what happened in a single digital visit. That's clearly essential, and we have no way to build a broader understanding of a digital journey without the ability to understand the individual components of that journey.

However, it's just not enough to be able to understand each digital visit. To really understand the digital world, we have to string together those visits into a broader journey. In the chapters on voice of customer, we focused on the ability to bring in outside behavior to understand what happened after a digital touch. Equally important, however, is the possibility of stringing together digital touches into a full journey that tracks a series of visits for a single visitor, as shown in Figure 9.1.

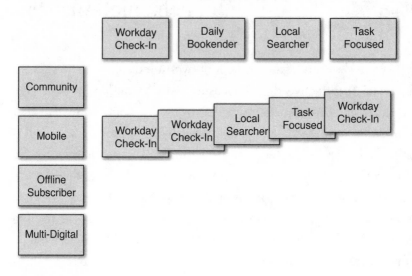

Figure 9.1 Tracking a sequence of visits

Understanding a sequence of visits by putting them together into one or more user journeys is a completely natural exercise in the digital world. It also resonates in the broader business world, where an increasing focus on the customer experience and the customer journey has helped drive the widespread adoption of life stage and funnel-based views of key business problems, such as customer acquisition and brand loyalty.

The two-tiered segmentation framework provides the fundamental building blocks to make this type of journey mapping successful. The visitor segmentation (the *who* tier of the segmentation) remains stable over the lifetime of most journeys. The visit segmentation (the *what* or use case tier) provides the building blocks of the journeys themselves. Because visit types reflect some combination of increasing levels of depth in a funnel (as in early-stage versus late-stage shopping) and fundamentally different types of activity (as in customer support versus shopping), they can be combined to represent multiple journeys or increasing depth in a single journey. Multiple journeys can be simultaneous or sequential. Journeys can be incomplete or successful. Indeed, these building blocks might even describe decreasing depth in a journey if a customer moves backward along the funnel. As with Lego pieces, when you have the right building blocks, you can connect them in an almost infinite variety of ways to represent all sorts of real-world journeys.

This chapter covers some of the techniques for combining the visits from a two-tiered segmentation into a full user journey—a kind of three-tiered segmentation. To do that, we'll use all the techniques outlined so far: the development of the basic visit segmentation, the addition of upstream and downstream events with voice of customer (VoC), and the importance of sequence, time, and pattern in understanding broader journeys.

The Myth of the Golden Path

Even back in the dawn of digital analytics, people understood how important sequence and pattern were to interpreting the digital experience. In fact, early practitioners might have had a deeper appreciation of sequence. Before we had easy, powerful software-as-a-service digital analytics tools, we used weblogs and traditional data-processing tools to try to understand digital behavior. In that world, it was easy to see how limiting SQL and many types of statistical analysis were when trying to make sense of digital behavior. We used to dream about the ability to actually see how users navigated a website. If only we could visualize the paths people took, we were sure we'd understand digital behavior at a much deeper level.

One of the virtues of our age is that if you have money and a problem, people will find ways to solve it for you. In this case, the solution came in the form of digital analytics tools. Those tools not only made it much easier to generate the kinds of simple, aggregated reports that most analysts were building in SQL, but they delivered powerful visualizations of how visitors navigated a web property (path analysis).

Being a DIY kind of guy (when it comes to software and analytics—I try never to touch any hardware more complex than a lightbulb), I wrote a customized C++ pathing program back in the early 2000s. It didn't have any fancy visualizations—in fact, it didn't have any visualization at all. But it did build a complete path analysis for a website and then spit out, by popularity, every single distinct path, how common that path was, and whether it had one of several key journey milestones inside it. At the time, we were working with a large brokerage, and it had given us a few weeks' worth of weblog data.

I still remember the anticipation as we first kicked off our pathing program against real data. And waited. And waited. And waited some more. Eventually, we killed it, added a bunch of debugging code, and ran it again. We realized that the program was going slower and slower because the number of distinct paths was getting very large very quickly. This is just the kind of thing that can kill performance on any computer. But clever programming or better hardware can nearly always solve performance problems. When that number topped more than a million distinct paths (for visits, not journeys), however, we began to realize that path analysis might not be the answer we were looking for. It doesn't matter how quickly you can process paths if you have too many paths to make sense of.

Our experience wasn't unique. Most folks waited for tools to create pathing visualizations instead of writing their own. But the experience was largely the same. The pathing programs that technology vendors eventually delivered were way better than my hand-crafted one in the way they presented the output. Unfortunately, pretty visualization didn't necessarily translate into useful visualization. Too many paths existed to be understood visually.

Eventually, the excitement over path analysis died away. It went from being an analyst's dream, to a key feature, to a checklist item, to something hardly even worth considering. If that sounds more like a sad movie about relationships, well, that's the way it often goes. Even with the most powerful path visualizations, most analysts found they simply weren't useful for solving real-world problems. This wasn't the fault of our technology vendors: They gave us exactly what we asked for. It just didn't work.

Back in the early days of digital, the most common questions digital analysts got asked were of the "golden path" variety. What's the most common path to purchase? What path do people take to register? What content solves this problem for users?

The idea was that if we just knew what content drove success, we could get rid of the rest and drive everyone down the same path. It was the sort of view, "I know half of my marketing dollars are wasted—I just don't know which half."

In general, this turned out to be mistaken.

It was mistaken partly because it missed the fact that most digital properties don't have a single function. No one path leads to success because there isn't one use case or one type of success.

Even within a single use case, however, the variety of paths visitors use to succeed are disturbingly varied. It turns out that people aren't all the same. They don't start with the same level of knowledge, interest, or qualification. Not surprisingly, this influences their behavior and their needs. The idea of the golden path isn't just an analytics mistake. It's a deeper mistake that occurs repeatedly in every type of endeavor. It's the assumption that people are the same, and it's an assumption that's often twinned with the even more mistaken proposition that everyone is "like me."

If marketing analytics works for any one thing, it's for avoiding this double mistake. A primary virtue of the two-tiered segmentation is that it forces everyone who uses it to embed the multiplicity of people and purpose deep into their thinking.

The deeper the mistake, though, the harder it is to kill. Path analysis has largely vanished from common digital analytics practice and the "golden path" question has become much less common, but the same mistake has re-emerged in the brave new world of omnichannel analytics. In omnichannel analytics, the goal is to stitch together a visitor's journey across a multitude of devices and touchpoints to optimize an entire experience. Websites, mobile apps, stores, call centers, and social networks all contribute specific experiences that combine to create the full customer experience.

Guess what the most common question is in omnichannel analytics? What's the best path for people to take across all these different touchpoints? And what technology solution is everyone looking for to do omnichannel analytics? The ability to stitch together the full customer journey to visualize the path!

This isn't going to work any better at the macro journey level than it did at the website level. The exact same lessons apply. Journeys are even less singular and monolithic in the omnichannel world than they are in the confined space of a website. People are different; their goals are different. And inside each use case is a multiplicity of paths that lead to any desired outcome. In omnichannel analytics, even more than in website analysis, there is no golden path.

The Implications

What are the implications of accepting that the idea of a golden path is a mistake? First, this shifts the emphasis of an omnichannel measurement framework from finding that path to understanding where visitors are (journey stage) when they arrive at a touchpoint and how that touchpoint can then best serve the journey. In other words, instead of trying to fit touchpoints into an idealized path, touchpoints need to be optimized for a wide range of tasks, given their unique characteristics. The goal of omnichannel measurement is to optimize the nodes for each customer, not the nodes for some idealized path. This approach harmonizes with the general philosophy behind the two-tiered segmentation. The goals and success of a digital property might not be identical with who visitors are and what they want to accomplish, but they do depend on this.

To optimize a digital touch in an omnichannel world, therefore, that channel needs to understand the intent of users when they *arrive*. This is very much a two-tiered segmentation question—but it's a question with a twist because it involves looking at all the previous touches as if they were a visit. In effect, creating a segmentation of users based on what they've done tells us where in their journey they likely are—what problems they have and what tasks they do most often.

Omnichannel Analytics: Journey Stage

The goal of omnichannel analytics is to understand a customer across multiple touchpoints in many different kinds of channels. With so many experiences spanning both digital and nondigital touchpoints, it's an important and necessary extension of digital measurement. VoC enabled us to bring up- and down-stream experiences back into the digital measurement foundation to help measure success. But omnichannel analytics is a different kind of problem. With omnichannel analytics, the goal isn't to bring nondigital data into the digital framework; the goal is to have a framework that covers digital and nondigital equally.

Can two-tiered segmentation be that framework, or do omnichannel analytics require a different or deeply modified framework to integrate digital and nondigital experiences?

We don't have much reason to expect two-tiered segmentation to be appropriate for omnichannel measurement. It was purpose-built for digital measurement. In its original conception, no consideration existed for how or whether it could measure nondigital experiences. Fortuitously, it turns out to be generalizable in a way that makes omnichannel analytics surprisingly akin to digital measurement.

In a two-tiered segmentation, the first tier is a traditional visitor segmentation. This segmentation should and does generalize across digital and nondigital. After all, the visitor segmentation is nothing more nor less than a traditional customer segmentation of the sort that's been used for countless business operations and marketing problems for the past 50 or more years. It captures customer relationships, customer demographics, life stages, and attitudes—whatever helps understand who the user is.

The second tier of the segmentation started out as unique to digital. The second tier is the visit/intent segmentation that captures what happened in a particular digital visit. Part of what makes this use case type of segmentation valuable is that it simplifies a complex set of behaviors into a few simple data points. A digital visit can range from one or two digital events (think page views most commonly) to a complex set of interactions that can include dozens or even hundreds of events—a mixture of page views, video streams, and control clicks—to sort, filter, or select data. Using this data in its native format is hard.

With a visit segmentation, however, all those events are effectively reduced to these few simple fields:

- Visit start time
- Visit type (web, mobile)
- Visit type (use case)
- Visit success
- Visit value

This then combines with the visitor segmentation to create a remarkably compact but powerful representation of digital behavior:

- Visitor ID
- Visitor segmentation

That's it: Just seven fields can usefully describe a visitor's digital interaction with a channel.

If a framework is going to work for omnichannel measurement, it's essential that every different type of touchpoint be represented in the same type of data structure. If different types of touches have fundamentally different types of data, combining them and using them in a consistent manner will be hard.

Perhaps because the use case segmentation had to deal with multiple channels (mobile and web) and many different types of digital touches (purchase, branding, entertainment, support, and more) right from the start, it is surprisingly adept at meeting this requirement. Call center data, for example, maps perfectly into this structure. One of the key data elements in the call center is the call purpose—which, of course, maps cleanly into the visit type field. Call centers also typically use a resolution code to reflect whether the call center visit was successful. It's trivial, therefore, to combine call center and digital data into a set of journey records mapped within a two-tiered segmentation.

Branch visits aren't much more challenging. There's nearly always a reasonable summation of what happened during a branch visit into a visit type, and there's also generally a good measure of success (task completion). It's true that branch visits tend to be more multifunction than digital touches. You can handle that by either forcing a primary visit type (a strategy that is surprisingly effective in bricks-and-mortar business) or embracing a unit of work philosophy and carving up visits into multiple touches.

Store visits are a little more challenging. First, store visits are typically recorded only with purchases (and returns, of course), making it harder to measure success versus failure. It's also harder to understand what a store visit was about. Ideally, it would be nice to understand when people visited a store for shopping and didn't make a purchase. This might be more possible with the widespread integration of mobile apps and loyalty programs, but for now, it's not uncommon for a store visit to be synonymous with a purchase. It's also a bit problematic that purchase visits tend to be classified under one use case. That need not be the way of things. Classifying market baskets might be a good means of creating multiple types of in-store use cases and potentially even creating sliding measures of success based on the type of basket at checkout. So although store visits aren't quite as natural a fit as call center interaction or branch visits in the two-tiered segmentation scheme, they work well enough. What's more, the problem isn't so much that the scheme feels unnatural when it comes to store visits; it's more that store visits don't typically collect some pieces of information that would be powerful and would nicely fill out the segmentation.

That's much more promising than if it feels as if the visits themselves somehow broke the paradigm.

Most semi-automated touchpoints fit easily and naturally into a two-tiered segmentation. ATMs, for example, naturally collect a visit type and a task completion (with a very high success rate). Voice response units (VRUs) also fit perfectly into the framework. Indeed, VRUs can be analyzed in a manner nearly identical with digital properties, with significant optimization opportunities. As with digital properties, VRUs almost demand to be understood within a two-tiered segmentation.

If a system that can cover every type of digital touch, branch visit, store visit, call to the call center, VRU, and ATM in one single journey framework is required for omnichannel analytics, two-tiered segmentation fits the bill.

Building the Measurement Framework for Tracking Journeys

Of course, just because a two-tiered segmentation can incorporate all these types of touchpoints doesn't mean there isn't work to be done on the underlying data. If a visitor comes to the website and then dials the call center, it's really important to understand whether the call focused on the same task as the web visit. If so, that means the web visit almost certainly failed. (Remember the customer support pattern in Chapter 8, "Big Data and Measuring the Digital World"?) The types of use cases described in the two-tier segmentation need to be standardized across every channel. Call center data and web data need to have matching visit types and purposes.

Every channel won't have exactly the same set of use cases, but when a task crosses channels, the use case must be described and categorized identically, as shown in Figure 9.2. Then it will be possible to track journeys across channels in a natural and easy-to-analyze way.

Figure 9.2 A sample customer journey

This type of progression shows how a shopping visit failure morphs into an attempt to update account information on the web, which then gets resolved in the call center and eventually loops back to a successful transaction: two different channels, three different types of visit, one common framework.

The process of building omnichannel segmentations is largely the same as the process Chapter 3, "Use Cases and Visit Intent," described for building intrachannel segmentations in digital analytics. Keep in mind, however, that what follows assumes that the work to do this inside each channel has been already done. In other words, before tackling an omnichannel segmentation, each contributing channel must have its own two-tiered segmentation that describes what a visit was about and whether it was successful. The output of all those channel-level models is then recombined at the visitor level to produce a new omnichannel segmentation using the same basic process (see Figure 9.3).

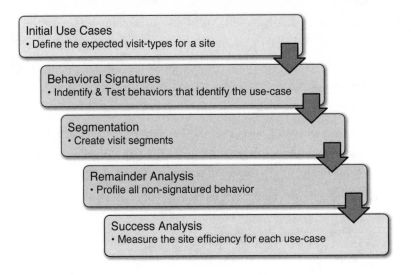

Figure 9.3 Building an omnichannel segmentation

Building the set of initial use cases can be ridiculously easy or pretty challenging, depending on how similar the omnichannel use cases are to the digital use cases. It's not unusual for a mature digital property to be a pretty substantial microcosm of the entire omnichannel system, but it's never going to be a perfect representation (at least, in an omnichannel world). The call center is a great source for additional use cases: It would be unusual for the call center not to contribute additional common use cases beyond those captured in the digital world.

As with digital use case development, using VoC to both bootstrap and validate a set of omnichannel use cases is entirely appropriate.

However, in omnichannel, you have the special consideration of where you conduct your research. Research in any channel naturally creates biases based on the users of that channel (web, call center, store, or branch). On the other hand, users in a channel are often the best people to survey because they are guaranteed to be engaged with the channel. If you've ever tried to solicit interesting comments about your website in an offline survey, you know how challenging this is. Unless someone is a really heavy user of a digital property, asking about it away from the moment of usage is probably hopeless.

The need to blend cross-channel information with in-moment depth means that VoC for omnichannel almost always has to be, itself, omnichannel. By standardizing the research program across channels, it's possible to combine the results from each channel into a comprehensive omnichannel set of use cases.

Incidentally, it's almost always a good idea in omnichannel VoC to focus on research using third-party websites and traditional offline techniques. Most omnichannel initiatives are at least partly geared to identifying gaps in the current ecosystem. Those gaps might not be visible if you survey only people who are active users of the ecosystem you've built.

Creating behavioral signatures for omnichannel customer journeys can be complex. Much depends on the number of channels in common use and the degree to which they support full functionality at each stage. Having omnichannel journeys that are as long as many web session journeys would be unusual, but the journeys themselves are often harder to unravel. It's also common to have multiple open journeys in the omnichannel world, which doesn't really exist when building visit-based use cases. Because of this, mutually exclusive segments aren't likely the right solution in the omnichannel world.

As the discussion around big data in the previous chapter probably made clear, identifying and classifying omnichannel use cases nearly always involves integrating sequence, time, and pattern. All of these are also present in building use cases for digital visits, but it's often possible to create simple proxies that don't involve more advanced analytic techniques. In a complex omnichannel situation, that's likely not the case, making omnichannel journey analysis one of the most analytically demanding tasks around. Not only does it require significant work on each data source to create the intrachannel use case classifications, but it then demands sophisticated analytic techniques to combine those intrachannel use cases into an omnichannel journey pattern to build the actual segmentation.

The process for doing omnichannel remainder analysis is pretty much identical to the process for creating use cases within a single channel. When you've created the segmentations for every journey you can identify, a significant number of visitors might not be classified in terms of their journey or journey stage. You can create a report that profiles these visitors; typically, that report counts the type of use cases they are classified as having (and their current success in those) by each channel. This can be indexical, showing how that count compares to the average visitor, but it's often sufficient simply to understand what tasks by channel are involved.

The final step, success analysis, is similar, but there are two significant differences. Success in a channel typically closes off all previous open or failed channel-specific outcomes in the same use case. That's different from a single visit analysis, where there aren't usually discrete failures and successes—there's only a final outcome. In addition, the presence or absence of a journey step sometimes changes the success outcome of a previous step. In other words, if a visitor had a failed web customer support visit around a task and then a successful call center visit, the journey is closed successfully. All the touchpoints in a single open use case are treated as having an internal success and one final disposition (success). In addition, if a web customer support visit is flagged as a success but is then followed by a call with the same task, its true disposition is probably a failure. That doesn't happen inside a single visit because individual actions inside a visit don't have a success state.

Recency/Frequency/Monetary (RFM)

Building a use case segmentation by channel does more than just provide a mechanism for combining all of a visitor's touchpoints into a journey. It also offers a way to bring one of the most powerful direct marketing constructs to bear on omnichannel analysis. The idea behind RFM has been around since the early days of direct response marketing. It's not a sophisticated modeling approach—it's really just the embodiment of a very simple idea: How recently, frequently, and successfully a customer has done something, is the best way to understand how likely that customer is to do it again. This might seem counterintuitive, and it doesn't apply in some situations, but it works in a surprisingly large number of cases. It may be true that if you buy a washer/dryer, you're out of the washer/dryer marketplace for a good long while. But catalogers realized long ago that most product categories are very different. For the vast majority of catalogers, the more recently they'd purchased from a catalog, the more likely they were to purchase from the next one. And the more frequently they'd purchased in the past, the more likely they were to purchase in the future.

In fact, RFM turned out to be so commonly predictive and valuable that storing RFM information about customers has become de rigueur with customer-focused marketing professionals. In digital, however, it has been challenging to use RFM metrics intelligently. The problem is that, with no framework for deciding why people visited, knowing how often they touched a digital property wasn't particularly informative. A recent and frequent visitor to the website seeking customer support is definitely not an attractive marketing prospect.

Of course, the two-tiered segmentation provides exactly that information. That makes it easy to aggregate RFM information by use case for each visitor. In Figure 9.4, each cell in the segmentation matrix contains the RFM data for a visitor. This makes it easy to track which visit types a customer uses most, which was used most recently, and which have been successful.

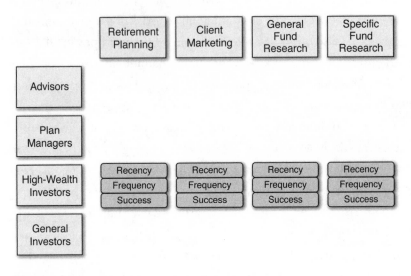

Figure 9.4 RFM inside a two-tiered segmentation

A single field can't always represent recency, frequency, or success. It often makes sense, for example, to store how recently an action occurred and how much time elapsed between the last two similar actions. Similar considerations can apply to success, as Figure 9.5 shows.

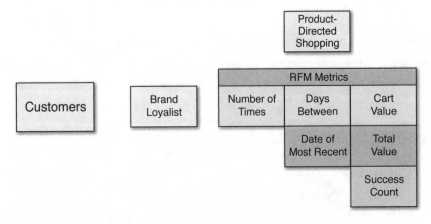

Figure 9.5 Adding detail to an RFM matrix

Saving how recently, frequently, and successfully a visitor has traversed each use creates a powerful picture of what a user cares about, how that is evolving, and where the user is not succeeding. It also puts this information into a powerful, easy-to-use form. With RFM stored by visitor in a two-tiered segmentation, you can easily create queries that get at a sequence such as "Find High-Value Customers whose most common visit type is Gift Buying and whose Most Recent Visit was unsuccessful" (see Figure 9.6).

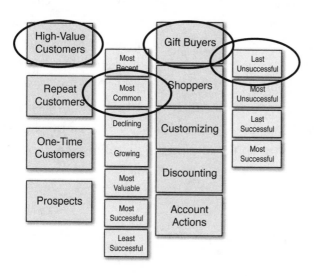

Figure 9.6 Targeting using RFM and two-tiered segmentation

That type of selection is nearly impossible to create against raw digital data. But if the analysts have done their work properly, even fairly unsophisticated users can easily select, analyze, and optimize across these critical RFM dimensions.

Omnichannel analytics extends the digital measurement framework to embrace a wide variety of customer experiences across many fundamentally different types of channels. The core of the digital measurement framework—two-tiered segmentation—has proven highly generalizable and appropriate to capturing the full customer journey and blending data from disparate sources. It's not as easy as it sounds.

Extending the framework demands separate but compatible use case classifications for every channel, a difficult exercise. After those individual channel segmentations are built, the omnichannel framework is then constructed in a relatively similar manner to the way use cases were built to measure digital visits. Instead of using page views, the use cases are built by stringing together each touch into a sequence. In effect, each channel touch made by a customer becomes the equivalent of a step (or page view) in the sequence. A key benefit of both the individual channel segmentations and the overall omnichannel journey segmentation is how easy they make it for people to consume the data. Instead of having to understand complex analytics, simple queries against journey stages and success are made possible. A prime example of this is the ability to create meaningful RFM metrics within the omnichannel segmentation and then make those metrics available for reporting and targeting. RFM is easy to understand and apply; for many types of targeting and optimization, it's a surprisingly good fit within a two-tiered, omnichannel segmentation framework.

10

No End in Sight

Don't think we've totally figured out how to measure the digital world. We're still at the 3R's level of learning—we're still figuring out how to see, measure, define, and interpret this cool new world. And of course, that world keeps changing. New digital paradigms challenge our measurement concepts and force us to continually rethink what we think we know. In this chapter, we revisit each step in our measurement foundation and show how it fits together to create a strategy for digital measurement. Then we finish up with some thoughts about where digital measurement is headed and some of the challenges new digital channels and behaviors will create.

I started measuring websites back in 1997 or thereabouts, almost 20 years ago. I'm the kind of person who gets bored easily, so it still surprises me that, after almost 20 years, my interest is still there. That's a tribute to how immature the discipline was back in the 1990s: Our main goal was to create the most inflated hit counts possible so that tiny startups could justify their absurd valuations to venture capitalists. Did that measurement ever stink! We were pathetically far from even beginning to understand how to measure the digital world. When you start off that far behind, it takes a long time to reach anything remotely like maturity. It's also a tribute to the rapid evolution of the digital world itself. The measurement problems the digital world presents have grown, changed, and morphed as new channels have emerged. Smartphones didn't just extend the digital world— they changed it, adding new complications and new types of behavior. The same is true for social communities, each of which presents distinct behaviors and data sources. New devices, new channels, and new tools have all added depth and interest to digital measurement.

Even better, the vastly increased importance of digital in our lives has created oceans of behavior and expanded the importance of integrating digital into broader customer journeys. As any analyst will attest, the more behavior there is, the better the analysis we can do. In the early days of digital measurement, websites were often content poor. We didn't understand the importance of metadata—but it wouldn't have mattered that much because the content wasn't good enough to classify. Certainly, we didn't realize how applicable voice of customer (VoC) was to the digital world. But because we didn't have any online survey tools, that didn't matter much, either. We weren't concerned with measuring call centers, ATMs, or stores. In fact, we knew that the measurement being done in those areas was vastly superior to what we could do in the digital world. Their disciplines were more mature, the physical tools were better, and their methods were flat-out better.

At the time, our goal was to make digital measurement equivalent to those other disciplines. But as the need for omnichannel measurement has become widely apparent, digital paradigms are proving the most robust. And it isn't hard to see why. The world is becoming more individual even as it becomes more impersonal. Optimization of experiences at the mass level is increasingly unacceptable in the digital world, and mass-level marketing is increasingly ineffective.

Digital measurement has always had the infrastructure to measure at the individual level, although it took a long time for the tools and the analysts to move beyond the measurement of assets (pages). Making that journey presented real challenges. The struggle to find ways to attach meaning to behavior has been long and difficult in the digital world—far more difficult, for example, than in the credit-card industry, where I worked before I became an Internet enthusiast. You have to work far harder to get meaning out of a page view than out of a purchase. In the long run, those difficulties have been good for digital measurement.

The challenge of making measurement meaningful when it's nothing but a sequence of behaviors forced digital analysts to understand the process of inferring meaning from consumption and the challenges presented by structure. It led to an ever-increasing focus on metadata to help weld meanings to underlying behavior. Even better, it forced the introduction and gradual incorporation of VoC concepts deep into the behavioral model. Perhaps in other fields behavioral and attitudinal measurement have become as deeply ingrained within a single methodology, but this fusion is unprecedented in the broad business world.

As is so often the case, the very real challenges of measuring the digital world forced the gradual illumination of better techniques. New techniques turned out to be significantly better than the old alternatives. Fortunately, those techniques have been very adaptable—we had no guarantee this would be the case. Certainly, no one was striving for measurement beyond digital when tackling these problems. Maybe the inherent complexity of the digital world resulted in measurement frameworks with a fairly high degree of adaptability—or maybe it was luck. Or maybe I'm merely overconfident in the success of this framework for omnichannel measurement. After all, it's still very early in this omnichannel endeavor.

Reviewing the Framework

The hardest part of measuring the digital world isn't mastering a particular tool. In fact, mastering a tool is exactly the wrong way to start. Digital analytics tools will most definitely not point a new user in productive directions. They encourage a kind of aimless "run this report, then run that report" style of measurement that neither informs nor deepens understanding. The real challenge in digital analytics is more basic. It's learning how to draw the connection between what's measured (a seemingly bloodless trail of digital consumption) and the people taking the journey. Doing this well certainly requires mastery of the data that describes digital behavior and whatever tool is used to track that behavior. Much more important, it demands the ability to understand those digital journeys and describe the content choices that identify particular journeys. Every digital journey is a constant balancing act between what a visitor wants and what content is offered. Understanding how those choices play out and which choices describe particular journeys is not merely an analytics exercise. It demands a deep knowledge of the digital property. Some analysts believe it's possible to fruitfully analyze digital behaviors without deep knowledge of the actual digital property. They are wrong. To build the bridge between metrics and people, knowledge of the territory traversed is absolutely essential.

As we have seen, at the heart of digital measurement is a two-tiered segmentation that classifies all visitors to a digital property by who they are and what they are trying to accomplish. This framework is the best way we've found to put flesh on the bones of digital measurement, to connect digital behaviors to the people doing them. It serves as a way to understand the success of a digital property, optimize specific experiences, drive personalization, and, ultimately, connect digital and nondigital touchpoints in a single journey.

The first step in building a two-tiered segmentation is to understand what types of journeys might be possible. Analysts who are deeply experienced in a particular property and its consumers might already have a deep intuitive sense of those journeys. When that isn't the case (or when validating that intuitive sense is important), VoC techniques can first identify why visitors come to a digital property and then map actual site behaviors into signatures for these purposes. Site walk-throughs are another technique for helping the analyst begin to understand the topography of a digital property and the types of behavioral cues it might generate.

With a set of potential journeys in hand, the next step in building a two-tiered segmentation is to create robust metadata on the content consumed. This step is absolutely critical to creating a rich segmentation. It's built on the most basic principle of all digital measurement: What people consume tells us what they want. The choices people make in navigating are self-selecting and indicate their true interests. To understand those choices, it's critical to understand, at every junction in a digital property, which choices were available, which were prominent, and which were chosen. Most important, it's critical to understand what those choices mean.

Metadata about content is data that describes key aspects of content, to help analysts understand who might choose that content and what it means if they do. No one right set of metadata exists for content, but common types of metadata about content include functional descriptions, topic taxonomies, intended audience taxonomies, sales stage classifications, role descriptions (what role a consumer might have to be interested), and data fields that describe how complex, image laden, and recent the content is. The richer the descriptions and the closer they track to the use cases and business, the better the segmentations they will produce. The process of identifying, testing, and building metadata about content never ends: We always have new ways to think about content and, particularly for content-rich sites, new types of metadata classification that can produce opportunities to expand or refine a digital segmentation. New classifications of content are often the single best tool for improving digital measurement.

With a core understanding of likely digital journeys and a rich set of content metadata to help map consumption to intent, it's time to create an actual segmentation. This process involves finding behaviors on the digital property that successfully predict that a visitor is within a specific use case. You create these behavioral signatures in many ways. Using the types of filter builders common in digital analytics tools, an analyst can construct a series of segments based on filtering rules. Alternatively, data-driven approaches such as clustering can weld together numerous digital behaviors and find logical group-ings that can then be mapped into the journeys they represent. VoC data can validate hand-built or data-driven rules, but an even more powerful approach is to use VoC visit intent as the target variable that behavioral variables are modeled to predict.

The choice between using a bottom-up, data-driven approach and using a top-down, rule-based approach is usually driven by tool and data access. Having deeper access and powerful statistical analy-sis tools to drive a bottom-up approach is nice, but it's far from neces-sary. Great measurement is possible with either technique. What's more, both methods rely on the analyst having a prior understanding of what content consumption means, what journeys exist, and which ones matter. The idea of pure machine learning is still largely illusory. When analysts describe a set of metadata, they implicitly make judg-ments about what's important and what types of segmentation are potentially interesting.

The two-tiered segmentation these methods produce classifies every single visit to a digital property. It provides a way to measure the distribution of visits to a digital property by use case and a framework for understanding what constitutes success.

The second great challenge of digital measurement rears its head at this point. Digital properties have structure. That structure is inten-tional—it's explicitly designed to steer visitors in specific directions. It also cues visitors to paths they might be especially ready to take. Digital visits are a challenging mix of visitor intent, self-selection via navigation cues, and construction of the digital property that is try-ing to influence the visitor to make specific selections. The less clear the navigation cues are, or the better the force is, the less visitors' behavior might indicate their real intent. Every digital visit reflects this complex balancing act. To understand what content works within a use case, analysts must constantly find ways to control for structure and self-selection biases that could overwhelm the measurement of both visitor intent and content effectiveness.

The offline world also first intrudes in the measurement of success. Standalone digital experiences do take place, but more often, a digital experience is part of a larger journey that includes multiple types of digital and nondigital touches. Experiences as diverse as talking to a call-center agent, navigating a voice-response unit (VRU), getting a piece of mail, visiting a branch location or an ATM, and going into a store can all be pieces of a single customer journey. When a journey isn't completed online, it can be nearly impossible with purely behavioral measures to decide whether that experience was successful. Two visitors with identical behavioral patterns could end up with completely different outcomes. A subjective rending of success in such situations leaves measurement and analytics as objects for debate, with any piece of bad news seen as evidence that the chosen measurement of success is simply wrong.

Here VoC provides a way to extend the reach of the measurement system. The idea of "ask before, ask during, and ask after" uses sampled populations to measure the prequalification of audiences when they arrive at the digital property and then resurvey to measure their downstream success. Stitching together the prequalification view, the actual behavior on property, and the resurvey data constructs a complete model of digital behaviors to offline success. This method enables analysts to answer fundamental questions about digital success that too often are left open, crippling the measurement process. In an effective analytics organization, measurement of success cannot be up for perpetual debate.

Finally, the measurement framework extends to omnichannel analytics. Having a common data framework is essential to analyzing a customer journey across different types of experiences. Having call center, branch, and digital data together on a single big data platform doesn't do an analyst much good unless there's a way to integrate that data in a meaningful fashion. Two-tiered segmentation provides just that method of classifying almost any kind of touch in a common framework for analysis.

In the analysis of omnichannel journeys, we are firmly placed in the "big data" world. This is the frontier of current digital analytics, where traditional IT and statistical analysis paradigms mostly break down. It's a world where order, time, and pattern are critical to a statistical understanding of what actually happened.

Omnichannel analysis starts with constructing channel-specific use case segmentations based on a common framework. The data is then combined and a full omnichannel set of use cases is constructed. The process for this omnichannel segmentation is similar to the process of building a digital specific segmentation—journey steps take the place of page views as the atomic elements of the analysis. After that full journey segmentation is built, the door is open for simplified access to meaningful customer data using metrics such as recency, frequency, and monetary/success (RFM).

That's the digital measurement framework. It's a way to understand the digital world, to translate the point measurements that the measurement infrastructure produces into a comprehensive view of what's happening in that virtual world. It's a way to tie metrics to people in an approach that deepens understanding and supports optimization and personalization.

Some Humble Time: All Things Not Covered Here

If you're interested in digital analytics, hopefully you've found the framework presented here exciting. It's so obviously more powerful and coherent than the "bag of tricks" approach to digital measurement that focuses on running particular reports and finding certain kinds of anomalies. Looking for down-and-back yo-yo navigation patterns, analyzing zero-result search terms, alerting on variations in site traffic—sure, that bag of tricks can be useful, but those tricks form no coherent method or approach. They find problems to fix, but they don't provide understanding. They are ends in themselves, not starting places for analysis. If you have a big enough bag of tricks, it can last for a while and make you seem pretty smart. Like any bag of tricks, though, it has a bottom—and when you reach that bottom, you'll run out of tricks. The "bag of tricks" approach is particularly useless when it comes to building teams and training analysts. If everyone works from the same bag of tricks, the bag gets empty really quickly. Worst of all, the approach fails at the single most important task of digital measurement: to create understanding. Understanding comes from measurement, and with understanding comes the ability to effectively communicate. A digital measurement framework is, as much as anything, a way to talk about digital properties in a way that makes sense of the digital world to the whole enterprise.

That's what the framework laid out here is designed to do. And yes, I think that's pretty great.

But a staggeringly huge amount of stuff isn't covered within this framework. Important stuff—really important stuff.

I've barely touched on whole areas of digital analysis. Except for some tips on using prequalification and resurvey to more effectively measure campaigns, little in this book addresses the gigantic set of problems involved in optimizing digital marketing spend. From mix, to attribution, to individual campaign optimization, I've skipped whole new types of analysis. Is two-tiered segmentation a part of digital marketing analysis? You bet it is. Understanding the mix of visitors sourced by a specific campaign—their prequalification, their use cases, and their success—is pretty darn critical. But it's by no means complete. These techniques are essential to measuring raw performance of individual campaigns. They don't cover the analysis methods necessary to extend that to optimization problems when multiple campaigns have multiple overlapping touches. Nor are they the "be all and end all" of campaign-specific optimization. Interesting campaign-specific techniques address tasks such as optimizing bidding situations in PPC and discovering sources of variation in advertising markets. These aren't part of the measurement framework here, though.

It's plausible to view digital marketing as almost a separate discipline from the measurement of digital properties that the measurement framework describes. Even within the realm of digital properties, however, the framework must be recognized as just that: It's a frame, not a complete picture. This book omits numerous important analytic techniques designed to solve particular problems in the digital world. I sometimes teach a class on the digital analytics toolkit that includes sections on two-tiered segmentation, functionalism, and VoC, all of which are richly covered here and are essential elements of this framework. But this class also has sections on topographic analysis for analyzing site structure, analytics for cohort analysis in social media, analytics for optimizing merchandising drives and product assortment, funnel analysis, and real estate analysis. All are fascinating and important topics within digital analytics, but I've given them little or no attention here.

Some areas, such as merchandising, live almost completely outside the framework but might be more important than anything else you do if you're working on an ecommerce site. Other areas, such as real estate analysis (which analyzes the appropriate amount of space to give site elements), are natural extensions of the framework presented here. Social media analytics (a huge and fascinating area in its own right) lives somewhere in the middle. Two-tiered segmentation and functional concepts have considerable utility in social media, but whole new relationships and methods in social media analytics are fundamental and completely new.

As with any rich field, plenty more books have yet to be written and untold lessons remain to be learned. The entire framework described here is no more than the concrete foundation on which a giant building waits to be erected.

Looking Forward: Where There's Still Work to Be Done

If I've left out that much, then there's much room for improvement and development in the foundation itself. The chapters on big data and omnichannel measurement highlighted the potential role for more advanced statistical analysis and data-driven pattern discovery and classification. This lives right at the heart of the measurement framework and applies equally to the development of the core digital two-tiered segmentations. The rule-driven filtering approach common in digital analytics tools puts far too much on the shoulders of the analyst, whereas clustering and VoC-driven logistic regression don't do enough to handle sequence, time, and pattern. The more complex the digital property, the more important this is. Either of the traditional approaches I've outlined capture simple properties with less complex behavior fairly well. Properties with complex behavior, though, are much more likely to have numerous patterns that are difficult to find or classify without fundamentally new approaches to the data.

That grab bag of tricks is another good place to look for opportunities. I suspect that the tricks in that grab bag are mostly our clumsy initial attempts to find critical patterns of digital behavior. Understanding that pattern matching is critical to digital measurement, clever analysts have found ways to pick out a small set of interesting cues that occur pretty commonly on different digital properties. Deeper application of statistical methods designed to do real pattern identification and classification will likely both extend and regularize this bag of tricks. Ideally, that regularization will come with a repeatable set of methods for finding and describing the key patterns of behavior on any digital property. This will truly be big data analytics.

We also need better approaches to modeling the kind of choice architecture that any digital property involves. In this book, I've focused on the importance of experimenting and controlling for self-selection with segmentation to handle the constant push–pull introduced by digital structures and the "forcing" that designers do to push visitors in specific directions. Surely there are ways to model this in a deeper manner. Some theory is just waiting to be discovered and applied in a radically more interesting way that's more appropriate to the digital world than anything we've yet tried.

Finally, the integration of VoC and behavioral data seems to me to be an area where much work remains to be done. In few areas are the practice we recommend and the apparent state of the industry farther apart. The vast majority of VoC programs hardly seem to get any value out of their efforts, and integration with behavioral data is either nonexistent or used only for the most basic exploratory analysis (looking at low-scoring sessions, for example). We need a much richer set of methods for integrating VoC and behavioral data and using the two together to solve research problems. Our blundering, behavioral-centric efforts have yielded rich returns in almost every direction we've explored with integrated VoC. This makes me think not that we are particularly brilliant, but that this combination is uniquely rich. There is much here of academic interest, but we should investigate numerous practical applications where this combination could yield important new work.

Measurement and All It Means

We measure things to understand them, for without understanding, there can be no improvement. In so many situations, we take measurement for granted. It is an unconscious inheritance of millions of years of evolution across many species. We all have a gift for measuring expressions, judging dimensions, and predicting motion, among countless other attributes of our world. These gifts are the result of measurement. Even in the physical world, however, formalizing measurement into method regularizes, deepens, and extends our understanding. In the digital world, we lack natural gifts and must depend on a set of tools that are evolving with all the rapidity our intentions can bring but are still plainly immature. We are still learning *how* to measure digital worlds, and we are still novices in the art. We have learned that, more than anything else, measuring the digital world is about measuring people. We care little about how robots navigate a website, but we want very much to understand who is using a digital property and what those visitors are trying to accomplish. Answering those two questions well involves a mixture of tools and method, inference and intuition. As has been observed many times, this is both an art and a science.

The goal of digital analytics is not description; indeed, the aim of *most* measurement is not idle description. Building digital worlds is inherently intentional. Every digital property is a creation with an often vastly complex architecture that embodies a set of decisions about what people might want and how to steer them in appropriate directions. Part of what makes digital measurement so challenging is that very fact: the push–pull between user intentions and the digital architecture. Without measurement sophisticated enough to understand that push–pull, we can never understand and improve a digital architecture.

No shortcuts help in building great digital worlds. It takes hard work, fine design, good engineering, and constant attention to how well that world works for all its different users. In most cases, it also takes a recognition that no one "right" experience exists—only the best experience possible for a given user who is understood as well as possible in that moment. The framework here is all about how to measure the digital world to figure out that best experience possible.

This is a search for truth, and as with all such searches, it turns out to be hard. The digital world, like the physical world, is complex. Simple answers don't exist. We don't have one perfect metric, one golden path, one right report. The world, digital or otherwise, just doesn't work that way.

However, certain methods do work. These methods can help measure when, where, and for whom a digital property is working well—and when, where, and for whom it isn't.

Figuring that out is a worthy endeavor when applied to any useful digital world. Using measurement to drive change is a way to make a bad digital world okay, make an okay digital world good, and make a good digital world great.

So go out and build great worlds.

Index

A

analysis
  experimentation versus, 143
  traditional versus digital data
    analysis, 207-215
analytics tools. *See* digital metrics
Angel's Taco Divina (ATD) food
  trucks example, 41-46
arrival articles (page type), 108
articles (page type), 108
ask before, ask during, ask after (VoC
  strategy), 175-176, 247
  offsite surveys, 182-184
  online surveys
    benchmarking and cross-site
      comparison, 191-194
    stability of, 188-189
    targeted surveys, 189-191
    types of questions in, 184-188
  prequalification measurement,
    176-179
  resurvey techniques, 196-200
    sampling bias in, 200-202
  success analysis, 194-196
  targeting precision, 179-182
ATD (Angel's Taco Divina) food
  trucks example, 41-46
audience taxonomies, 94-95

B

A/B tests. *See* controlled
  experimentation
background of digital metrics, 241-243
before-and-after analysis, 137-138
behavior. *See also* visit intent
  mapping, 122-124
  predicting, 90-91
  website structure and, 119-125
behavioral proxies in downstream
  value measurement, 199-200

behavioral segmentation, 245-246. *See*
  also voice of customer (VoC)
  building segmentation rules,
    154-160
  closed list versus open-ended
    questions, 147-149
  coloring with VoC data, 149-151
  future of, 252
  in omnichannel analytics, 235
  validating with VoC data, 151-153
behavioral shifting, 120-122, 131-133
  controlled experimentation and,
    133-139
behavioral signatures, creating, 56-63
benchmarking, 191-194
bias
  online surveys and, 171-175
  in resurveys, 200-202
big data
  digital data as, 203-207
  Four V's, 205-207, 218-220
  lack of measurement tools, 220-221
  in omnichannel analytics, 235-236,
    248
  use cases, 216-218
brand engagement in success criteria,
  76-79
brand knowledge of users, 54
brand value questions (online
  surveys), 186
broadcast shows, streaming shows
  versus, 168-169
brokerage sites (two-tiered
  segmentation), 32

C

call center conversions, website
  visitors and, 167-168
campaigns, optimizing, 179-182,
  249-250
car analogy (functionalism), 101-103